Can We Solve the Migration Crisis?

Global Futures Series

Jacqueline Bhabha

—————

Can We Solve the Migration Crisis?

polity

First published in 2018 by Polity Press
Reprinted 2018

Polity Press
65 Bridge Street
Cambridge CB2 1UR, UK

Polity Press
101 Station Landing
Suite 300
Medford, MA 02155, USA

ISBN-13: 978-1-5095-1939-2
ISBN-13: 978-1-5095-1940-8(pb)

A catalogue record for this book is available from the British Library.

Library of Congress Cataloging-in-Publication Data

Names: Bhabha, Jacqueline, author.
Title: Can we solve the migration crisis? / Jacqueline Bhabha.
Description: Cambridge, UK ; Medford, MA : Polity Press, 2018. | Series:
   Global futures | Includes bibliographical references and index.
Identifiers: LCCN 2017035018 (print) | LCCN 2018000320 (ebook) | ISBN
   9781509519439 (Epub) | ISBN 9781509519392 (hardback) | ISBN 9781509519408
   (pbk.)
Subjects: LCSH: Emigration and immigration--Social aspects. | Emigration and
   immigration--Government policy. | Emigration and
   immigration--Psychological aspects.
Classification: LCC JV6225 (ebook) | LCC JV6225 .B53 2018 (print) | DDC
   325--dc23
LC record available at https://lccn.loc.gov/2017035018

Typeset in 11 on 15 pt Sabon by
Servis Filmsetting Ltd, Stockport, Cheshire
Printed and bound in the United States by LSC Communications

For my Rafa and Sebas, our future

Contents

Acknowledgments

Writing a very short book on a topic one has spent one's whole life working on is no easy endeavor. Communicating one's distilled thoughts cogently and accessibly, without the customary academic toolkit of footnotes and technical language, is, if anything, even more challenging. If I have managed to overcome these hurdles, it is thanks to most generous help along the way: intelligent research assistance and constructive criticism from colleagues, friends, and family.

I am grateful to my students Lauren Windmeyer and Alexandra Lancaster for their assistance, and to Faraaz Mahomed for the unusually fine research support he so consistently provided. Colleagues at the Fletcher LLM Seminar, Princeton, the University of Connecticut, York University in Toronto, the Center for Migration Studies, a Bellagio Seminar

Acknowledgments

on Global Migration Law, and Rutgers have all helped refine my thinking. Courageous migrants and refugees as well as dedicated migration activists working within the UN system and in NGOs on the frontlines of human distress have continued to fuel my strong sense of the urgency to do more and better.

My Harvard colleagues at the Carr Center for Human Rights Policy, the Weatherhead Center for International Affairs, the Graduate School of Education, the Department of Global Health and Populations at the T.H. Chan School of Public Health, and above all the FXB Center for Health and Human Rights offered invaluable feedback on early drafts and inchoate ideas. Close friends and family, including Ana Colbert, Nancy Cott, Michal Safdie, Oliver Strimpel, Homi, Ishan, Satya and Leah Bhabha, provided insights, suggestions, and encouragement without which I would still be lost en route to my destination. Finally, I am indebted to insightful peer reviewers and an exceptionally fine editorial team whose clear vision helped develop my own.

Preface

The rate of contemporary migration is staggering: 24 people are forced to leave their home every minute. The cumulative scale of this global displacement is equally dramatic. At 65.3 million, the population of forcibly displaced people exceeds that of the UK, of Canada, of Argentina, of Australia, and of Kenya. If this displaced population were a nation, it would be the 21st most populous in the world.

Because the modern world is divided up into states with borders and a strong interest in controlling the entry of non-citizens, this large-scale, unregulated migration has become a global political priority of the first order. It continues to dominate both international and domestic agendas. It has severely affected one of the most promising political innovations of the postwar period, denting free movement within the European Union, perhaps irreparably, and unleashing virulent xenophobia across the continent. It has dramatically impacted political leadership, contributing to the precipitous fall of UK prime minister David Cameron, and to the surprising victory of US presidential candidate Donald Trump. And it has altered the political bargaining power of whole countries – Turkey most obviously, despite that country's rapid descent into authoritarian and undemocratic rule. Even the increasingly nationalistic and commercially driven world of global sports has taken note. Setting a world precedent, the standard bearer during the opening ceremony of the 2016 Olympic Games was not a national representative but a refugee, a member of the first ever Refugee Olympic Team.

It is not just the scale and rate of current migration that attract attention, but the wide-ranging, and, until recently, unimaginable responses. In 2014, who would have predicted that Germany would admit more than 1 million asylum seekers, becoming within a year the de facto conscience of Europe? Or that EU member states would erect razor wire fences where free border crossing had been the norm, painfully evoking Europe's darkest hour? Or that a single, unforgettable image of a drowned 3-year-old Syrian, with relatives in Canada ready to sponsor him and his family, would lead a guilt-ridden young president to dramatically increase his country's refugee resettlement figures overnight? Or that a newly elected US president would attempt to legitimate explicit religious discrimination in immigration admissions and bar entry indefinitely to refugees fleeing one of the most murderous civil wars in decades?

Many of these developments have faded from the headlines with the passage of time and the advent of yet more human tragedy and political instability. But it is the apparently irresolvable nature of the refugee and migration problem, and its ramifications for the contemporary geopolitical order, that continue to provoke a sense of anxious panic and drastic reactions among policymakers and voters alike. At the same time, with vicious conflict raging, and dramatic political and economic inequality plainly evident for all to see, migration, however dangerous, presents itself as one of the few available exit strategies for millions. For both sets of affected constituencies, we need to ask: do better alternatives exist and, if so, what are they?

To answer these questions, I propose to pursue four avenues of inquiry. First, when do population flows constitute a "crisis" rather than the ebbs and flows of normal migration fluctuations? Are there previous episodes of massive population movement and related migration panics that provide instructive historical data points for the present set of challenges and dilemmas? Second, taking a step away from history and politics, what do we think ought to happen – or, more broadly, how do we evaluate the ethical issues raised by the current situation? What do we consider the entitlements and the claims on ourselves, our governments, and our common resources of populations to whom we are either completely or largely unrelated? Conversely, what moral entitlements if any should members of a community have to determine their own composition, and to restrict access to outsiders seeking to live within their midst? Joseph Carens, a prominent ethicist of migration, presents the repudiatory treatment of Jews fleeing Nazi Germany as an extreme and, he presumes, unacceptable consensus limit case for exploring available options. Unless we have a sense of what spectrum of alternatives might count as "fixing" the refugee and migration "crisis" and what strategies would fall outside that defined field, we cannot satisfactorily resolve the question.

Third, I will outline central elements of the legal and administrative framework that states apply to movements of people across international borders. This will cover both official responses to forced movement, including refugee and humanitarian flight, as well as state policies toward migration that is considered "voluntary," often referred to in contrast to refugee flight as economic migration. Finally, I will consider the main drivers of contemporary forced migration[1] and positive and workable strategies for the future. This will involve consideration of issues beyond the field of migration and refugee management per se. I will suggest that no viable or just resolution to current refugee and migration pressures can be sustainably reached without addressing the factors that drive people to leave home, whether temporarily or permanently. Measures to reduce distress migration will fail, in the medium and long term, without attention to legitimate quests for greater social, political, and economic equality. I will outline some ingredients of this far-reaching reform program and tie them to some of the initiatives currently being undertaken.

1

A Crisis Like No Other?

In Chinese, the word "crisis" is formed with the characters for danger and opportunity. This captures some of the duality at stake in use of the word – a moment of threat that introduces pressure to innovate. Crisis discourse features in many contexts – political, economic, organizational, personal. Among the different glosses on "crisis," two are particularly relevant to migration. Laura Henderson suggests that the purpose of crisis discourse is to dislocate existing narratives, substituting a new narrative that offers solutions: tackle danger by discarding current remedies in favor of new ones.[1] A second approach analyzes crisis-driven rhetoric by reference to three key actors: a responsible villain, an affected victim, and a resolving savior. While the villain causes a crisis for the victim, the savior intervenes to resolve the situation, taking advantage of the need for action to generate the consensus needed to drive change.[2]

Reactions to recent migratory events have deployed some of these narrative strategies. The notion of "crisis" has become ubiquitous, a shorthand for marking the unique features of the present and the legitimacy of radical measures to address them. I will argue that current circumstances are not unique, and that instead of quick fixes focused on migration (essential though some such measures are), we need to develop an integrated approach to the factors that propel large-scale distress migration. A historical perspective on human mobility contextualizes current pressures within the long-standing ebb and flow of complex human migration patterns. This perspective offers precedents for anticipating and addressing the multiple ripple effects of movements of people that we are seeing today.

Lessons from History: A Brief Overview of Migration's Longue Durée

By contrast with dominant contemporary accounts of the refugee and migration crisis, migration history encourages us to think of human movement as being separate from the act of border crossing.[3] This history demonstrates, across a broad canvas of time and space, that the factors affecting human mobility have been remarkably constant over centuries (indeed, over millennia). Equally constant is the range of mechanisms for responding to this mobility, mechanisms characterized by power asymmetries and self-interest. Historical, linguistic, and archeological evidence suggest that only where migrating populations have brought with them superior technical abilities or unknown germs have their arrivals posed fatal threats or long-term security challenges to the settled population.[4] This is a useful corrective to the inflated rhetoric of civilizational crisis often invoked in connection with contemporary migration.

To point out that "people have always moved" is to state the obvious. In a well-known book, Benedict Anderson noted more than 30 years ago that nations are "imagined communities," cultural products of individual human endeavor and collective organizing rather than facts about any inherent or permanent link between place and people.[5] They are also recent inventions, as are the borders that define them.

Our species, *Homo sapiens*, first emerged from Africa about 150–200,000 years ago. Genetic and archeological scholarship now confirms that an "African Eve" was "the mother of all humanity."[6] The movements of early human groups were determined by the evolving ability to exploit two large clusters of natural resources, those generated by water (lakes, rivers, seas, oceans) and those generated by soil. The imperative to secure means of survival and to adapt to changes and opportunities in one's environment has always been a fundamental driver of human mobility. From the earliest traces of history, human migration and its interaction with increasingly diverse physical and climatic environments, at the water's edge and inland, contributed to dramatic breakthroughs and the diffusion of new animal and plant breeding techniques. Survival, innovation, and ambition continue to be drivers of human mobility.

The impact of early resource-expansion advances on migration was complex. On the one hand, the move away from hunting and gathering toward an agrarian economy associated with the obligation to till the land and tend to herds of animals encouraged a sedentary lifestyle. Then, as now, the overwhelming majority lived out their lives in one place (even today, only 3 percent of the world's population are international immigrants). On the other hand, then, as now, the destruction of traditional agrarian livelihoods prompted out-migration of communities.

By 3000 BC, crop cultivation had expanded rapidly to cover previously uncultivated areas, generating a growth in population size and, with it, the potential for conquest, commerce, and exploration. Pack animals facilitated transport of people and of substantial goods for purposes of commerce. So too did the development of new forms of aquatic transport, including sail- and oar-propelled vessels. By 2000 BC, human migration had extended to all inhabitable spaces.

Archeological and historical evidence suggests that, as now, young travelers were mainly those forging links with new communities, absorbing previously unknown techniques, languages, and habits as they expanded their spheres of operation. Fascinating DNA-related archeological research illustrates the complex human movements now encoded in skeletal remains, food from different regions leaving an indelible trace of migration trajectories.[7] It generates a detailed picture of the syncretic products of multiple migration-facilitated interconnections over time.

One can think of these movements as evidence of growing global exchange or of progressive regional or continental division. The conclusion depends on the baseline against which human mobility is measured.[8] Historically, as now, long-distance migration separated families and led to economic, social, and cultural divergence from the original community and changes within the new society. But it also generated new connections, and did not always interrupt old ones. Economic, military, and political factors combined in different ways to generate connection or separation, integration or division, just as they do today.

Four Broad Drivers of Migration Across the Ages

A helpful typology identifies four broad and non-exclusive drivers of human migration over a very large historical canvas. These provide a simplified and schematic backdrop for contextualizing present-day challenges and assessing whether our current migration situation is one of exceptional "crisis."

Historian Patrick Manning points out: "Migration of whole communities was usually a *migration of desperation* rather than hope ... refugees driven by drought or conquest." The 20th century, as we will see, provides numerous examples of this first driver, a form of desperation-driven migration, where only those too old or too sick are left behind. Throughout human history, people have fled their homes to survive.

In the absence of such desperation, populations tended to be more selective. When sufficiently confident, they used a second strategy, migration to colonize, a process that included both temporary and permanent migrations, and flows in multiple directions. By the first millennium BC, Indo-European and Semitic speakers began domesticating horses and using them to draw chariots and carry warriors. These developments led to a significant innovation in military conquest capability with radical political implications across Eurasia and south to the Indian peninsula. Civilizational consolidation led to massive construction projects – of pyramids, temples, roads, and waterways – which in turn fueled the mobilization of large numbers of laborers, many of them enslaved. Over 10 centuries, from the 5th century BC to the 5th century AD, conquest-fueled migration gave rise to empires, from the Han Dynasty in China to the Roman Empire across the Mediterranean and into North Africa. With construction came fortification – and the first walls used as early devices for excluding outsiders from cities or other settlements, a technology still in favor today.

In the Americas, Peru developed a highly central-
ized empire in the Andes in the 9th century AD,
dominating neighboring peoples, forcibly resettling
some and importing others as seasonal workers for
major construction projects such as the building of
Cuzco, which employed 40,000 laborers for a span
of 10 years. From the 15th century onwards, British,
Spanish, Portuguese, Dutch, Russian, and Japanese
colonization remodeled continents for generations,
leading to the extraction of raw materials, to devastating epidemics that decimated native populations,
and to ruthless local exploitation; it also led to new
trade routes, new forms of production and commerce, and rich and complex variants of social and
cultural exchange between colonizer and colonized,
patterns that shaped and still shape contemporary
migration flows.

These were large-scale migrations for the times.
For example, close to half a million Spaniards traveled to the Americas between 1500 and 1650. Spanish
and Portuguese colonization of the Americas led to
dramatic population changes – disease and conquest
reduced the population of the Mexican peninsula
from approximately 25 million to 2 million over the
period of one century, a "near genocidal" impact
that dwarfs any contemporary consequences of
migration. Centuries later, in the 19th century,

with the move toward agrarian capitalism in Latin America primarily fueled by coffee and banana production and the development of railways, large-scale intra-continental migration took place, compounding the forced dislocation of native peoples. In these contexts, migration-fueled "crises" or harms were the consequence of domination and exploitation by powerful over less powerful groups, not the reverse.

Similar processes of contact-induced illness, brutal conquest, and forced relocation decimated North America's native peoples. Agricultural developments and the need for exploitable labor fueled further violent forced migration, of brutally enslaved African populations. Concurrently, further south, silver mines in the Andes became the site of violent relocation of native peoples as labor fodder for a burgeoning global trade. Chinese migrants also participated in this trade, bringing Asian laborers and traders into this intensely globalized picture, a forerunner of vast Asian expatriate communities today.

The colonial migrations, even when the numbers of recorded colonizer expatriates were small (according to the 1891 Census of India, only 100,000 Britons were estimated to be living in India), generated enduring legacies, not only for the natives and the migrants, but also for future links between colonizing and colonized populations.

9

A Crisis Like No Other?

Well into the 20th century, large-scale recruitment brought millions of colonial laborers to distant territories. Following the abolition of slavery in 1833, Britain began exporting South Asian workers across its empire – to Mauritius, Guyana, Trinidad, South Africa, and Fiji. By 1916, more than 1.5 million Indians had been shipped out to the Caribbean, Africa, and Oceania. Over the next 20 years, a further 6 million Indians were recruited to work in plantations in Malaya and Ceylon, seeding one of the largest and most extensive global diasporas of all time.

Whether these migrations were "coerced" or "voluntary" is contested. What is clear is that the migrants, many of them temporary workers, were often severely exploited, generating the backbone of imperial accumulation rather than personal wealth. This historical legacy is relevant both to the ethics of modern migration control and to the impact of global inequality, issues discussed in later chapters. Although the era of imperialism is largely over by the 21st century, economic and cultural domination associated with extraction of raw materials, control of markets, inequitable trade agreements, and unsustainable debt persist.

Large-scale migration between colonizer and colonized did not stop with the end of empire. The

reverse migrations of formerly colonized populations to the metropolitan homes of their erstwhile
exploiters – captured by Paul Gilroy's felicitous
phrase "the empire strikes back" – have been substantial. These constitute a third type of migration,
migration driven by the quest for a better quality of
life. From the mid-18th century to the latter half of
the 20th century, immigrants to the UK overwhelmingly came from the colonies. Large numbers of
Indians started migrating to the UK after Indian
independence in 1947: more than 60,000 by 1955,
and yet more after Indian UK passport holders from
East Africa left to escape from increasing racial discrimination. While some moved to improve their
business prospects, others fled persecution and
expulsions following decolonization in Kenya and
Uganda. Spain became an immigration destination
country much later than Britain or France, but even
there the scale of postcolonial migration has been
considerable. Between 1996 and 2010, approximately 2.5 million Latin Americans moved to Spain
and became Spanish citizens.

These reciprocal human movements, retrac-
ing the footsteps of colonizers but without their
predatory or coercive mission, provoked periodic
migration panics akin to today's crisis-fueled discourse. There is, perhaps, no clearer example of the

inflated rhetoric of crisis, even apocalypse, to justify immigration restriction than the famous "Rivers of Blood" speech delivered by British Conservative MP Enoch Powell in 1968 in response to nonwhite immigration from Britain's recently exploited Commonwealth. "It almost passes belief," he proclaimed, "that at this moment 20 or 30 additional immigrant children are arriving from overseas in Wolverhampton alone every week . . . Those whom the gods wish to destroy, they first make mad. We must be mad . . . It is like watching a nation busily engaged in heaping up its own funeral pyre . . . The sense of being a persecuted minority . . . is growing among ordinary English people . . . As I look ahead, I am filled with foreboding; like the Roman, I seem to see 'the River Tiber foaming with much blood'."[9] Some of today's anti-immigrant rhetoric is likely to seem as preposterous half a century on.

A fourth, broad migration category, neither solely refugee flight nor colonization, nor driven by the quest for a better life, though related to and on occasion overlapping with all of them, is immigration driven by the desire to further trade and commerce. With the creation of metallic coins as currency in both Roman and Chinese empires in the first millennium BC, a system of global commerce began to take shape. This early form of globalization depended, in ways analogous to contemporary movement, on an interconnected set of technologies – from increasingly sophisticated and reliable means of long-distance transportation on land and sea to the development of common trade languages enabling the building of trust. Eventually, however, peaceful mercantile trade gave way, during the 15th and 16th centuries, to military backing for commerce, which ushered in European and North Atlantic dominance, as Asia and Africa's role as drivers of global trade declined, a legacy with enduring and devastating contemporary consequences for global inequality, political stability, and related migration flows.

Together, these human migrations dating back thousands of years enabled exposure of early human communities to new resources, challenges, and rewards. Rarely present in their pure form, the four types of migration have combined and recombined in different ways across the expanse of time and space covered by human mobility.

Massive and Global Population Movements: Centuries of Continuity

As globalization spread across the early modern world, no region remained isolated or intact, no sizeable territory populated by a single unchanging tribe or people. Industrialization and the accelerated human exchanges it generated led to dramatic flows of population over the major sea masses – the Atlantic Ocean, the Southeast Asian Seas, and the Indian Ocean. Over four centuries, starting in the mid-15th century, somewhere between 10 and 28 million Africans were forced into slavery across continents by European, American, and Middle Eastern traders, with millions dying during the inhuman transportation process. Other forms of forced migration compelled very sizeable populations of indentured laborers from India, China, and elsewhere (including forcibly exiled convicts, and indigent or orphaned children) to work in far-flung places, from the railways in Uganda to the sugar plantations in the Caribbean. Forced mobility was, in these cases, followed by enforced immobility – both backed by legal bondage and armed force.

At the same time, and rapidly escalating from the mid-19th century until the advent of fascism in Europe, millions chose to leave home to improve their quality of life and future prospects. According to Patrick Manning, this massive outflow of migrants from Europe combined with huge numbers of Chinese (more than 50 million), Indian (30 million) and other Asian laborers and fortune-seeking entrepreneurs to generate unprecedented human movement (in excess of 100 million people). "Overall, the period from 1850 to 1930 was the most intensive era of migration in human history."[10] This history contextualizes current notions of a refugee and migration "crisis," with a scale of migration that dwarfs contemporary flows.

This dramatic mobility spanned the globe, including three major frontier destinations. More than 50 million people traveled from Europe and the Middle East to the Americas, as did sizeable numbers from India and China. Roughly similar numbers traveled from South Asia and South China to Southeast Asia, Australia, and the Indian and Pacific Islands. Nearly 50 million people moved from Northern China, Russia, Korea, and Japan to Central and Northern Asia, and as far afield as Siberia.[11]

Rapid social and political change in China in particular was responsible for massive population movements. From the end of the 19th to the middle of the 20th century, approximately 46–51 million people moved from Northeast China to Manchuria, and from a broader area to Japan. Meanwhile, about 1 million Chinese moved across the Pacific to the Americas, until they were blocked. The first formal immigration law banning an entire national group, the Chinese Exclusion Act, was enacted by the US in 1882.

Nationalism, Racism, and Border Control: The Advent of Modern Migration History

This period of massive human migration – the dramatic 19th-century rate increasing even further in the 20th century – was a continuation of early patterns of movement across communities. Even as very large-scale mobility across extensive distances was occurring, so border restrictions and increasing regulation of migrants through passport control were beginning to take shape – the US 1875 Page Act, which prohibited the entry of immigrants deemed "undesirable," is an early example.

In Europe, too, states strengthened their borders to control the large population movements precipitated by the collapse of European empires. Over time, the trajectories changed. Whereas the Caribbean had been one of the largest recipients of migrant flows between the 16th and the mid-19th century, it became a major exporter of population one century later.

These processes consolidated different layers of national affiliation. Large population movements of community members resulted in the formation of diasporas, generating dual or multiple (or what we now call hyphenated) identities. These populations were tied both to their current national location, but also to an erstwhile home, whether geographically, religiously, or ethnically defined. Migration, by vastly increasing the connections and cohabitations of different groups over centuries of movement and interchange, contributed to the exponential multi-plication of possible identities. But migration also contributed, along with many other factors, to the pressures to constitute nations and, within them, nationals with a distinct identity determined by that nationhood.

Between the end of the 18th and 19th centu-ries, the process of creating independent sovereign nations rapidly gathered momentum. Examples include the US (1776), Haiti (1804), Mexico (1810), Honduras (1821), Brazil (1822), Belgium (1830), and the UK (1899). In some contexts, the process of replacing multinational and multicultural empires with nation-states took the form of forced popu-lation transfers, attempts to create homogeneous national spaces with populations mapped neatly onto territory. These processes fueled the develop-ment of racism and the promotion of unconditional adherence to one's "nation." "To belong, migrants

– and resident minorities – had to change cultures, to 'assimilate' . . . [requiring] unconditional surrender of pre-migration ways of life."[12]

Until the late 19th century, no state passed laws imposing immigration control. This of course did not mean that human migration was completely unfettered. The major impediments were initially technical and logistical (means of transport, availability of supplies) and then, as "empty" habitable space vanished, they became social and political (exclusive land ownership, religious conflict). By contrast with contemporary wrongs, historically by far the largest abuse in matters of human migration was not forced exclusion or removal from national territory but, rather, the forced importation of enslaved or indentured populations. Population imports or increases were generally considered mechanisms for enhancing wealth, productivity, and power. Conversely, population loss from emigration or colonizer resettlement was generally considered to be detrimental to national heritage and labor potential, unless those leaving were considered undesirable (convicts or orphans, for example).

All this changed – at first gradually and then ever more dramatically – with the advent of the 20th century. The development of racial stereotypes and eugenicist thinking fed into political demands for race-based migration restriction. In close succession, within less than 25 years of each other, first the US (in 1882) and then the UK (in 1906) introduced immigration control laws restricting the entry of particular populations.

The historical and economic contexts were different – the US legislation targeted Chinese workers seen as competition with the domestic labor force, while the UK legislation targeted Jews fleeing pogroms in Eastern Europe. But the rhetoric was remarkably similar – the imperative of excluding immoral migrants belonging to inferior races. The US Chinese Exclusion Act had a dramatic impact. Whereas 20–35 percent of Chinese migrants between the 1850s and the 1870s went to the Americas, contributing, inter alia, to the construction of the first ever transcontinental railway, the proportion dropped to between 2 and 5 percent after 1890. (It took 80 years and the passing of the 1965 Immigration and Nationality Act for US immigration policy to rid itself of explicit discrimination against Chinese migrants.)

So, a precursor of future patterns, it was not human mobility per se that was the target of the first immigration control policies, but a racially defined subset of migrants. Over time, northern governments developed increasingly comprehensive and rigorous migration laws designed to restrict and carefully control the entry and stay of non-nationals. Only after World War II did national reconstruction in the Global North require a massive injection of migrant labor to supplement decimated national working-class populations.

The Migration Consequences of Ethnic Separation

The massive population movements of the early and mid-20th century, with millions forcibly displaced by two world wars, are by now a matter of history rather than of personal recollection. During a single decade less than a hundred years ago, the 1940s, enormous refugee and migration flows took place. In the early and mid-1940s the Nazis forcibly displaced 7–9 million Europeans, and the war as a whole led to the displacement of more than 60 million people. Later, Jewish settlement and related political developments forced out approximately 85 percent of the Palestinian Arab population of what eventually became modern Israel.

Just two years after the end of World War II, another population exchange of dramatic proportions and humanitarian import took place when the British partitioned the former jewel in their colonial crown into two new nations, (primarily Hindu) India and (predominantly Muslim) Pakistan. The attempt to divide a formerly multi-ethnic and multireligious imperial territory on the basis of religion left massive numbers of people on the "wrong" side of the new and artificial border. Barbarous butchery of the minority community on both sides of the divide cost more than a million lives. Between August and December 1947, some 15 million people were forced to flee, leaving behind their homes, their assets, their monuments, and their history – a clear example of a migration of desperation.

Once again, repeating ancient history and prefiguring contemporary realities, each family and each individual had to balance competing equities and make the choice about whether or not to leave. As so often, the most prosperous and well connected left first, followed by the able and skilled. The proportion of those from the poorest, unskilled agricultural communities to leave their homes was smaller – only 40 percent of the Hindu refugees who fled from East (Pakistani) to West (Indian) Bengal were peasants, even though they represented 75 percent of the erstwhile Hindu population in East Bengal.[13] By 1956, less than 10 years after Partition, according to the government of India's statistical survey, a third of all refugees were fully employed, representing a higher rate of employment than the local population.

Extermination, expulsion, border control, encampment, and forced relocation all featured in these dramatic human movements, leaving a powerful personal, social, and political legacy. In all these situations, as in more contemporary contexts, immobility or the impossibility of movement, rather than migration, produced the greatest existential threats to populations.[14]

While these early 20th-century displacements are not common currency today, many do recall more recent displacements of people, which should place the contemporary migration and refugee "crisis" in perspective. As recently as the 1970s, extensive population dislocations occurred in several regions across the globe. One dramatic instance was when, in the early 1970s, roughly 10 million people were displaced as a result of civil war in Pakistan, a legacy of the earlier Partition of India and a conflict that eventually gave birth to Bangladesh. The scale of this outflow and the regional response are instructive as a comparison with current refugee outflow challenges. Between April and December 1971, approximately 100,000 people per day fled into India, leading that country to construct (with the help of the UN High Commissioner for Refugees

– UNHCR – and of the International Committee of the Red Cross) 330 refugee camps. No wall or razor fence was erected. Approximately 6.8 million refugees lived in camps and another 3 million were accommodated by Indian host families across the country. All refugees were registered by the Indian authorities as they crossed the border and were given an entry document, a special food ration for their inland journey, and anti-cholera and small-pox injections. By contrast, many Syrian refugees hosted in neighboring countries today lack registration documents, while declining vaccination rates in refugee camps have led to outbreaks of infectious diseases such as cholera, unknown to this population before the Syrian conflict erupted.

Shortly after the division of Pakistan, in the mid-1970s, upheavals in Southeast Asia following the end of the protracted Vietnam war and the establishment of communist regimes led to refugee movements of more than 3 million people, this time from Lao, Cambodia, and Vietnam. Approximately 800,000 so-called "boat people" fled to Malaysia, Indonesia, Thailand, Hong Kong, the Philippines, and elsewhere in the region; an estimated 400,000 perished during their journeys.

Massive continuing outpourings of refugees from Vietnam to other Southeast Asian countries prompted the latter to threaten the closing of their borders and to insist that Vietnam prevent out-migration. However, neither strategy – border closure or blocking exit – worked, a forerunner of future repeated failures on both these fronts. Eventually, the UN Secretary General was able to broker a deal whereby Vietnam prevented "illegal" or unauthorized exits and instead undertook to promote forms of "orderly" departure. Simultaneously, other countries agreed to accept a greater share of responsibility for the desperate refugees leaving their countries by significantly increasing their resettlement rates. By 1979, Indonesia and the Philippines were accepting 25,000 refugee resettlements per month and, further afield, Western countries, including the US, Australia, France, and Canada, accepted well over half a million resettled refugees between 1979 and 1982, a figure that dwarfs current refugee resettlement rates. A global responsibility-sharing program, responsive to the humanitarian crisis playing out in the aftermath of the Vietnam war, saved and improved the lives of millions of destitute refugees. Again, this constitutes an instructive set of precedents for contemporary challenges.

Despite these valiant efforts, by the late 1980s there was still no end in sight to the exodus of

Vietnamese refugees. Very significant numbers of people, whole families and communities in fact, remained intent on fleeing the policies of the Viet Cong government. This led to forced internal relocation, re-education camps, and other radical government containment measures. By this time, however, attitudes toward refugee resettlement in the region were changing, as governments, fueled by domestic pressure and the absence of workable international agreement, were no longer amenable to the sustained responsibility sharing of the previous decade. By 1987, Thailand began intercepting and returning Vietnamese refugees (this return was technically known as "refouling" from the French "refoulement," or return to a place where there is a risk to life or liberty). Prefiguring contemporary political reactions, Western countries also reversed their earlier more generous entry policies, arguing that fleeing Vietnamese were "economic migrants" rather than bona fide refugees. This was the precipitating context that led to the Comprehensive Plan of Action introduced in 1989.

The Plan was instituted to encourage repatriation of Vietnamese refugees and to reduce resettlement numbers for the benefit of Western countries. It did not work. Refugee flight from the communist regimes in Southeast Asia continued. Eventually, agreement was reached with the Vietnamese authorities, who established an Orderly Departure Program for those seeking to leave, avoiding perilous and undercover sea journeys. Resettlement figures continued to rise, with the US, recognizing its contribution to the devastating fall-out of the conflict and the resulting human rights obligations, resettling 1 million Vietnamese refugees. Many of the drivers of massive forced migration, the strategies adopted by the refugees, and the responses of states are forerunners of what happens today. The current European refugee "crisis" exemplifies a well-worn historical trope.

At the end of the 1970s, conflict in Afghanistan precipitated yet another massive population displacement. This displacement was first fueled by the Soviet, Cold War inspired, invasion of that strategically positioned mountainous country. But the disruption of Afghan life was exacerbated by other events: the rise of the Taliban, the US invasion following the World Trade Center bombings of September 2001, and, concurrently, catastrophic environmental disaster caused by drought. One result of these calamities has been the flight of nearly one-third of the country's 26 million citizens. By the beginning of this century, more than 8 million people had fled Afghanistan, the vast majority hosted in just two neighboring countries, Pakistan and Iran. Despite some cessations of hostilities and refugee returns, by 2013 more than 7 million Afghan refugees were still displaced outside their country. To this day, with Taliban and other radical militant activity constituting an ongoing and significant danger and nearly half a century of conflict stalling national reconstruction, Afghans remain among the most numerous of asylum applicants in the European Union (EU). The devastating impact of prolonged conflict and a failure to systematically address its human, economic, and political impact will scar Afghans for generations to come.

Massive displacement during the second half of the twentieth century was not just the product of non-European events. The disintegration of the Soviet communist empire at the end of the century led to several episodes of large-scale forced migration. The first, during 1991, was the exodus into Italy of hundreds of thousands of Albanians, fleeing the collapse of their brutally oppressive government and the ensuing political chaos. Prefiguring contemporary maritime arrivals on Italy's coasts, thousands arrived on crowded vessels and had to be accommodated in makeshift lodgings, including in the Bari football stadium. Even more impactful in terms of both scale and political urgency was the refugee outflow related to the bloody conflict that broke out following the breakup of the Socialist Federal Republic of Yugoslavia. Between 1992 and 1995, about 100,000 people died and well over 2 million were displaced, by far the most devastating European humanitarian crisis since the end of World War II. Though Bosnian Muslims suffered the worst fatalities and violence, including numerous and barbarous incidents of rape and pervasive targeted "ethnic cleansing," very large numbers of Serbs and Croats were also affected. The huge displacement of populations provoked a complex, often restrictive set of migration policies, a precursor in many ways of responses that have characterized the current crisis. Two similarities are particularly noteworthy. European burden sharing was nowhere in evidence, leading Germany to accept a disproportionate number of asylum seekers. Second, instead of granting permanent refugee status to the desperate forced migrants fleeing for their lives, many European states introduced forms of temporary and subsidiary protection, a more precarious kind of humanitarian assistance, that eventually, after peace was signed, led to swift and harsh deportations of newly settled communities back to their war-torn homelands.

A Crisis Like No Other?

Some Historical Take-Aways

This sketch of migration history demonstrates the ubiquity of mobility, as a strategy of survival and self-advancement. Over the millennia, human beings have traversed enormous distances, defying physical and cultural boundaries, and forging new connections as they have maintained old ones. The longue durée perspective on human mobility challenges the "crisis"-driven approach to contemporary migration. It shows how large-scale migration flows over time change the baseline against which the scale and importance of the "invasion" or "flood" are measured. Human mobility has generated dangers – for native populations, for colonized peoples, for exploited migrants themselves – but it has also produced dramatic opportunities. Political, cultural, economic, and ethical priorities have combined in different ways to influence the flows and the perceptions of these dangers and opportunities. English Puritans who arrived in New England as refugees from religious persecution became American founding fathers and citizens, but decimated the Native American population. Indian and Chinese migrants chasing economic opportunity in the distant Atlantic became Caribbean or African or Latin American, intermingling with local populations and spawning hybrid identities and cultures. Greek-speaking Muslims forced out of Salonika in the Balkans as a diplomatic quid pro quo for the displacement of millions of Christians in Anatolia became members of a newly secular Turkey.

The response to arrivals of newcomers involves many variables, as does the decision to migrate: a complex and often speculative weighing of advantages and disadvantages – economic benefits, cultural challenges, political fears, human costs and gains. The language of crisis obscures this time-worn complexity by imposing a fixed and dominant framework – the perceived threat to the already present community – over the many other critical and relevant variables, including the possibility of social and economic enrichment, of local and geopolitical enhancement, of interconnectivity and technological gain. All these dimensions include imponderables. Among them are questions of ethics, the duties, if any, that we owe to others, some of whom we may have oppressed in the past. How far do or should such obligations extend? And what consequences do or should they imply?

2

A Duty of Care

On September 2, 2015, a watershed event took place. Nilüfer Demir, a Turkish journalist, photographed the lifeless fully dressed body of a 3-year-old Syrian boy, Alan Kurdi, washed up face down on a wet beach near the fashionable Turkish sea resort of Bodrum.[1] The toddler's family of four had paid a fee of $5,860 for the half-hour crossing between Turkey and the Greek island of Kos, their third attempt to start the long journey to Canada. All members of the family were wearing the fake life jackets routinely provided by smugglers to their clients, fakes that suggest, but do not deliver, protection. Thousands of these jackets now line the floor of the Mediterranean Sea, flanked by remains of the lifeless bodies they covered. Five minutes after the family boarded the small rubber inflatable in the dead of night, the boat capsized. Two other children also died in the same tragedy. More than 12,000 refugees and migrants trying to reach Europe have drowned in the Mediterranean since early 2015. If safe and legal migration routes had been available to them, none of these people would have lost their lives.

What, if any, are our moral obligations to distress migrants fleeing for their lives? And to the many others whose harsh home circumstances lead them to migrate? Do we have an obligation to share our privileges? Are we justified in putting our personal or national self-interest first? Is sincere fear a legitimate basis for discriminating against some populations? Is there something about the collectivity we call a country that justifies assertions and concomitant protection of a national "identity"? Is generous humanitarian aid to support needy others, provided they remain outside our borders, an adequate response?

These anxious questions have a direct bearing on whether and how we can solve the refugee and migration crisis. The migration history discussed in Chapter 1 shows how interconnected human populations are and how constructed rather than "natural" the association of people and place is. Nevertheless, many constituencies firmly reject obligations to strangers both inside and outside their countries, advocating isolationism, stepped-up border enforcement and militarily enforced blockades. Several vocal political constituencies have called for this, on both sides of the Atlantic. President Trump has repeatedly boasted that, thanks to his property development credentials, no one can build a border wall more effectively than he can: "I will build a great wall – and nobody builds walls better than me, believe me – and I'll build them very inexpensively. I will build a great, great wall on our southern border, and I will make Mexico pay for that wall. Mark my words." An opposing viewpoint comes from those who call into question the moral legitimacy of restrictive border control, and advocate instead a much more generous set of border crossing policies.

At issue in all these approaches are our moral identity, the solidarity claims it generates, and the justificatory principles driving those claims. Are our obligations to others, such as they are, best understood in terms of their proximity to us (physical, cultural or spiritual) or in terms of the intensity of their need (economic, medical, political); in terms of our giving capacities (material wealth, stability of our democratic institutions, national population density) or in terms of other ethical mandates by which we make meaning of our own lives?

These questions implicate us as individuals. But they also inform issues of distributive justice and questions about how, as political communities (cities, states, regions), we implement our collective ethical commitments. Answers to questions about our duties to "others" are about both hospitality and solidarity, about who we welcome or allow in to our collectivity (the immigration question), about how we treat migrants already physically in our midst (the nondiscrimination question), and about what we owe needy "others" far from our home (the global equity question).

I will suggest that the moral compass we use to address our obligations to strangers at home must apply, however modified or attenuated, to strangers from outside. Citizenship or nationality are not predetermined contracts for reciprocal support among a closed group, but affiliations that generate duties and entitlements the scope of which the collective defines and redefines. No a priori justification exists for a particular remit. We are all part of the process of definition and redefinition and accept outcomes we disagree with at our peril (or shame). We might sympathize with strong loyalty to, even psychological dependence on, embedded cultural traditions, linguistic heritage, or the elusive national "way of life." But we must recognize how all these "facts" of social life are ever changing, living traditions rather than archeological relics.

Relevant ethical questions span both humanitarian obligations to protect and distributive obligations to share within and across territorial boundaries. I will suggest that, across cultures and religion, our spiritual and ethical traditions rely on an inclusive humanitarian foundation. Our normative inheritance, a response to cataclysmic events and histories of oppressive domination, encourages generous engagement with others. Our affective instincts, molded by enduring global exchange, drive a nondiscriminatory approach.

In multicultural and mixed societies, built through the morally neutral accident of birthplace and inward and outward migration over centuries (what sociologist Michel Foucault has called "the era of the side by side"), the very notion of "our society" requires scrutiny. Who worked the fields, generated the raw materials, and built the infrastructure and the industries that have made rich countries prosper? Past histories and lasting imbalances in trade agreements suggest powerful obligations of restitution for the enduring consequences of conquest, exploitation, and hereditary privilege. These histories are part of our ongoing present. Who services our daily lives and cares for the sick, the elderly, and the very young in wealthy societies today? Who makes our cars, our clothes, our computers? Who are we? The notion of "our society," of "us," is a construct that does not easily map onto culture or nationality, or fit comfortably within state borders.

Appealing to Emotions: A Polarized Response

The image of Alan Kurdi spread around the world like wildfire, fast and far. Within a few hours the picture went viral and, under the hashtag "humanity washed ashore," became the most tweeted item on Twitter.[2] Like the iconic and equally voyeuristic photograph of another child taken 43 years earlier, 9-year-old Vietnamese Phan Kim Phúc running naked after being severely burnt by a South Vietnamese napalm bomb, it was an image that would haunt a generation, perhaps changing the course of history.[3] And, like the earlier photograph, it provoked a set of sharply polarized emotional responses, with opposing answers to the ethical questions raised.

On seeing the photograph of Kim Phúc, the US president at the time, Richard Nixon, in a conversation with his chief of staff captured on an audio tape, reflected: "I'm wondering if that was fixed." Viktor Orbàn, prime minister of Hungary, responded in like mode to the picture of the Syrian 3-year-old. On September 4, two days after the toddler's death, Orbàn refused to be blackmailed: "We think all countries have a right to decide whether *they want to have* a large number of Muslims in their countries. If they want to live together with them, they can. We don't want to and I think we have a right to decide ... I do not see any reason *for anyone else to force us* to create ways of living together in Hungary that we do not want to see."[4] The "we" invoked by Orbàn is ethnically homogeneous, white, and Christian, engaged in a civilizational clash with Muslims. Hungary proceeded to erect kilometers of razor wire fencing, blocking free movement in the continental EU for the first time since the creation of the Union. At the same time, Orbàn's popularity shot up in the polls.

Brexit was the first major political consequence of the profound and widespread popular rejection of obligations to needy strangers voiced by Orbàn. As 2016 moved into 2017, a fear of terrorists, together with protectionism over domestic jobs and welfare benefits, generated a fertile soil for xenophobia and racism, with Islamophobia in the lead, but other hatreds increasingly legitimated.

No one has voiced this more eloquently than Donald Trump, providing global leadership to unapologetic endorsement of national self-interest and out-group scapegoating. The logic of refugee and migrant exclusion has increasingly become a central campaign demand that plays well, not just in Eastern Europe or rust belt America, but also across the old EU. A breed of political leaders – like the Dutch Geert Wilders, the French Marine Le Pen, the German Alice Weidel, and the Italian Beppe Grillo – have attempted, with varying success, to build a broadly based platform for a sharp "them and us" polarization that rejects duties toward outsiders and justifies narrow self-interest accompanied by stringent border control.

Many public statements issued immediately after the Kurdi drowning articulated a sharply contrasting view, expressing searing personal grief and an urgent sense of heightened collective responsibility. Nicola Sturgeon, leader of the Scottish National Party, captured a widespread reaction: "I will be far from the only person reduced to tears last night at the picture of a little boy washed up on a beach. That wee boy has touched our hearts. But his is not an isolated tragedy. He and thousands like him whose lives are at risk is not somebody else's responsibility; they are the responsibility of all of us." The day after Alan's death, Manuel Valls, then prime minister of France, put the same sentiment more telegraphically: "He had a name: Aylan Kurdi. Urgent action required – a Europe-wide mobilization is urgent."[5]

Jean-Claude Junker, President of the European Commission, spoke for many European leaders immediately after Alan's picture circulated. "Since the beginning of the year [2015], nearly 500,000 people have made their way to Europe. ... The numbers are impressive. For some they are frightening. But now is not the time to take fright. It is time for bold, determined and concerted action by the European Union, by its institutions and by all its Member States. This is first of all a matter of humanity and of human dignity. And for Europe it is also a matter of historical fairness. We Europeans should remember well that Europe is a continent where nearly everyone has at one time been a refugee ... [The situation] requires a strong effort in European solidarity. Before the summer, we did not receive the backing from Member States I had hoped for. But I see that the mood is turning. And I believe it is high time for this. ... Europe is the baker in Kos who gives away his bread to hungry and weary souls. This is the Europe I want to live in."[6]

The powerful ethical and religious resonances of this emotional speech are clear. They have been evident in the outpourings of human compassion and generosity accompanying the recent mass arrival of needy strangers in Europe. From free water bottles on offer at railway stations, to a refugee Airbnb organized among host families in the Netherlands, to a vibrant, publicly funded German Facebook site for refugees, to the loud proclamations of sanctuary city status by mayors and councilors across the US, the collective civic response to the arrival of destitute distress migrants has been dramatic.

Public support for refugees has not just taken place after their arrival. Many have contributed significant resources, economic and personal, to providing aid in refugee camps in the Middle East, and to enabling refugee resettlement through co-sponsorship schemes. In Canada, for example, private personal engagement with, and financial support for, refugees has implicated hundreds of thousands of citizens. Alan Kurdi's image sparked a huge outpouring of support: within a year of its publication, Canada had resettled more than 40,000 refugees, of whom over one-third had private sponsorship.

A Duty of Care

In God's Image: Religious Attitudes to Our Duties to Strangers

From Orbàn to Juncker, politicians commenting on the refugee and migration crisis have invoked religious and ethical beliefs. This is not surprising. Ineffable questions about the boundaries of hospitality and our duties to strangers have been at the heart of religious reflection from the dawn of theistic inquiry. Among the major Abrahamic texts, the Torah, the Bible, and the Qur'an, in their different ways, all describe a vulnerable stranger as either God or an instrument of God. But all the major religions also evidence a dramatic disjunction between scriptural text and quotidian practice. Although their doctrines mandate hospitality, regimes whose foundational authority is closely tied to religion rarely conform in their everyday policies.

The Bible provides one of the most compelling accounts of our obligations to strangers. The expulsion of Adam and Eve from Eden and their journey into the land beyond have been considered the original image of God in whose likeness *all* humans are created. Those who reject migrants because they are "not us" violate this common heritage. As the well-known passage from Leviticus (19:34) explains: "But the stranger that dwelleth with you shall be unto you as one born among you, and thou shalt love him as thyself; for ye were strangers in the land of Egypt: I am the Lord your God."

The New Testament too provides strong support for the simple injunction to "Love your neighbor as yourself" (Luke 10). Perhaps, following this injunction, some church officials have interpreted the notion of neighbor broadly, seeing in the holy family of Nazareth, fleeing into Egypt, the archetype of every refugee family. Islam also celebrates the obligations owed to strangers. Asylum seekers and refugees are entitled to protection under Hijrah law throughout Dar-al-Islam (the world where Islamic law applies) whether or not they are Muslims.

All these religious principles converge around a moral norm of unconditional hospitality, a norm whose practical implication is that – whatever the unknowns that strangers bring – they should be welcomed. Today, this norm – though also espoused by prominent contemporary philosophers such as Emmanuel Levinas and Jacques Derrida – seems utopian (i.e., belonging to a u-topos, a non-space). But this is because we are so myopic, so limited by and tied to the immediate present. The long history of human migration, as we saw in Chapter 1, shows how just being a needy stranger is an element in so many histories. All three primary Abrahamic religions, in the lives of protagonists such as Moses (rescued from the bulrushes), Jesus (born in an animal stable to parents in flight), and Muhammad (a refugee from Mecca), capture and translate the insight that "there but for the grace of God go I" into a strong tradition supporting both the nobility of the "journey" and the important place of refuge.

The precise parameters of the religious injunction to extend hospitality to the needy stranger are, in practice, much less clear than the norm of hospitality itself. The founding of Israel illustrates the problem. Though the quote from Leviticus motivates the commitment to welcome those who flee harm, the prioritization of Jewish sovereignty and survival as central aspects of the Jewish narrative and end goals in themselves have justified sharply restrictive policies not only toward Palestinians (within and without Israel), but also to other needy strangers seeking hospitality.

The application of Christian doctrine is also fraught with inconsistency. In the famous New Testament parable, for example, although the Good Samaritan provided aid, shelter, and support to the roadside victim, he did not take him home. Does that mean that the Christian obligation to refugees is satisfied by providing humanitarian aid abroad rather than resettlement in one's own country?

Some, including leading Western refugee advocates and scholars, have proposed this as a pragmatic and politically feasible compromise between intolerable indifference and unworkable idealism. If generous funds are provided to countries close to the source of distress migration, the argument goes, then refugee outflows and all the personal dangers and suffering, as well as the political consequences they generate, could be avoided.

I am not persuaded by this justification for large-scale refugee exclusion from the affluent North, an exclusion that contributes significantly to the current sense of "crisis" and seems to legitimate the perpetuation of vast inequalities in life fortunes. We see the enduring legacy of encampment in the huge refugee settlements in Dadaab, Kenya, where three generations of Somalis have now lived their entire lives without employment or future prospects, and in the de facto refugee prisons on the tiny, arid, and remote Pacific islands of Nauru and Manus, where Australia outsources its humanitarian hospitality. Camp life inevitably becomes a form of "bare life," a place of survival but little more, a denial of the opportunity to enjoy freedom and self-reliance.

Judaism and Christianity are not the only major world religions whose ethical edicts on the treatment of strangers have led to problematic outcomes.

The same is true of Islam. Although some predominantly Muslim states, such as Lebanon, Turkey, Jordan, and Pakistan have cited Islamic prescriptions to explain their open-door refugee policies, other Muslim countries have refused to allow access to refugees.

The contrast is stark. A verse from the Qur'an celebrating hospitality to strangers was prominently displayed between the two minarets of one of the most important and largest Istanbul mosques during the Eid (New Year) celebration in 2014, at a time when thousands of destitute Syrian refugees were arriving. Today, Turkey hosts more than 3 million refugees, the largest such population in any country. Saudi Arabia hosts no refugees. But like the good Samaritan, it has provided aid externally – over $700 million according to the Saudi foreign ministry, for school supplies, food, and medical provision. According to a 2016 Amnesty International report, other rich Arab countries – Qatar, the United Arab Emirates, Kuwait, and Bahrain – have also not admitted refugees.

Arab states rebut these claims. According to its government, Saudi Arabia has admitted 2.5 million Syrian refugees, but classified them as workers rather than as refugees because the country is not a signatory to the UN Refugee Convention. UNHCR reports that at least 500,000 Syrians in Saudi Arabia are classified as "Arab brothers and sisters in distress." In September 2016, the government of the United Arab Emirates announced it would admit 15,000 Syrian refugees over the following five years; in the same month the Amir of Kuwait reported that Kuwait had hosted 130,000 Syrian refugees, a figure equal to nearly 10 percent of the total population of Kuwait. So Islamic principles do seem to have influenced the region's border control policies to some extent. A Gulf state commentator rebutted European criticism of the region's humanitarian record: "European and US officials shedding crocodile tears over the plight of Syrian refugees are to blame ... [They should face] their shortsighted policies and welcome more Syrian refugees."[7]

Several major, non-Semitic religions also address the duties owed to strangers. Taoism, widely practiced in China, recognizes both hospitality and balance as virtues, since all human beings are children of Mother Tao, but balance has been interpreted to entail "moderation" in the admittance of refugees, a mandate for qualified rather than unconditional hospitality. One might suggest, however, that China has followed the injunction of moderation to an extreme, sitting on the sidelines as the Syrian humanitarian tragedy has unfolded.

At the end of August 2015, a year during which just under 1 million Syrians had fled their country, and nearly 5 million altogether were displaced, China, the second largest world economy, was hosting just 9 refugees and 26 Syrian asylum seekers.[8]

Buddhists value empathy, compassion, and generosity as important ideals, and, given the cycle of reincarnation, believe most people have, in some life, been a refugee. However, they recognize that ideals are rarely if ever fully realized. Politics – and thus refugee policy – are not directly considered as Buddhist responsibilities, but that does not mean that Buddhist religious thought is irrelevant to this domain. The obligation is to engage in adequate reflection and awareness of the prime importance of empathy before embarking on the policymaking process. This obligation does not appear to have been met by Thailand, a devoutly Buddhist country, known to enforce harsh, even inhumane measures on Burmese Rohingya fleeing persecution in neighboring Myanmar, and on other refugee populations in its midst. In 2015, about 100 asylum-seeking Uighurs, a persecuted Muslim minority in China, were subjected to months of oppressive detention in Thailand before being forcibly returned to a severe fate in China.

Several African ethical traditions also engage with

questions of hospitality. Ubuntu, a form of Southern African indigenous humanism, places the good of the community above self-interest – proponents suggest that this conception of a moral and spiritual need to act in the interests of others is central to the treatment owed to "outsiders." However, South Africa's recent harsh and exclusionary treatment of refugees, which attracted international attention following brutal attacks and summary deportation of desperate Zimbabwean refugees in the spring of 2015, calls into question its continued adherence to this philosophy. Another widespread African ethical tradition is Ujamaa, a philosophy of "extended familyhood." This approach characterized the way in which Tanzania responded to migrants and refugees during the heyday of pan-Africanism under Tanzania's first, and visionary, postcolonial government; refugees and asylum seekers were considered "resident guests" and welcomed. Today, this generous spirit is much less evident, as Tanzania foregrounds the strategy of national self-interest and cost-sharing that has spread across the historically hospitable African continent.

Thus, despite the prominence of hospitality toward strangers as a core obligation in all major schools of religious thought, clear religious edicts collide with the practical operations of state sovereignty and personal and national self-interest. While some avowedly religious states, such as Pakistan, Iran, and Turkey, have been generous with their hospitality to strangers, others – including Hungary, Thailand, the US, and the Gulf States – have not, often performing worse than more secular states such as Canada and Sweden. Although religious belief provides a strong basis for our duties to strangers, that belief needs greater political heft to significantly redress current migrant distress and need.

Non-theistic ethicists have also wrestled with the tension between public or private self-interest and the duties we owe others. Do their arguments strengthen the basis of our obligations to strangers?

The Forces of Reason and Emotion: Philosophical Approaches to the Ethics of Hospitality

In the 1980s, at a time when global distress migration flows were much less newsworthy than they are today, the philosopher Henry Shue made the following observation: "The world is full of foreigners. Most of them are strangers to me, and I have every reason to doubt that most of them have ever given me a thought. Is there some reason I should give thought to them?"[9] Though his concern is not specifically about migration and the regulation of borders but about the more general obligation to provide for needy others, his reflections and the analogies he uses to answer his question are pertinent to the consideration of what we owe strangers.

Shue writes: "An almost irresistibly natural-seeming image dominates much thinking about duties. We often see our duties from the point of view of a pebble dropped into a pond: I am the pebble and the world is the pond I have been dropped into. I am at the center of a system of concentric circles that become fainter as they spread ... My duties are exactly like the concentric ripples around the pebble: strongest at the center and rapidly diminishing toward the periphery. My primary duties are to those immediately around me ... plainly any duties to those on the far periphery are going to diminish to nothing, and given the limited resources available to any ordinary person, her positive duties will barely reach beyond a second or third circle."

Shue is right. It does seem "almost irresistibly natural" to assume that one's duties are strongest to those closest by – one's nuclear family, one's best friend, one's neighbor of many years. But do our duties, like the concentric ripples from the pebble, become progressively weaker the further away we get from what is closest to us? Do we owe more hospitality and material support to strangers in Europe if we live in the UK or Germany than we do to strangers in Syria or Afghanistan or South Sudan? Many would argue that we do. The EU and other regional agreements such as MERCOSUR (in Latin America) or ECOWAS (in West Africa) are based on this principle of proximal solidarity.

Shue disagrees. He sees no reason for greater obligations to nearby than to distant strangers. Duties, he argues, do not decline progressively with distance. Instead of concentric ripples, he suggests another picture: an irregular spider web with some short strands and some long strands. Unlike a short strand that fizzles out quickly, touching a long strand can have an impact on the farthest side of the web. With a phone call or bank transfer, the grant of a visa or a tele-medicine skype call, we might be able to have a life-saving impact on a needy stranger far away.

But, Shue argues, because this scope of potential impact is overwhelming, even debilitating, for individuals, we have delegated our duties to institutions – our government, Oxfam, Save the Children, the UN, the World Bank. These institutions cover the strands for us. If there is a long strand that connects a needy stranger to us, we have, through our political agency, to ensure that the institutional implementers act on their obligations, so that they carry out our moral duties for us. On this view, the strength of our moral obligations to strangers is not a function of their physical proximity to us; it is our ability to contribute to their well-being that is determinative. This is a compelling and, to my mind, persuasive account – our common humanity requires, at a minimum, that we engage with strangers to the extent that we can assist without ourselves being overwhelmed. For rich societies like ours, this sets a low threshold for engagement.

However, the tools we have to ensure the necessary institutional accountability need scrutiny – how do we delegate the obligation to deliver the hospitality we consider ourselves morally committed to? A dense web of civil society organizations and traditional and social media, together with systematic mechanisms for monitoring performance, can provide a strong starting point for evaluating institutional performance in real time. We have an obligation both as citizens and polities to invest in these tools to ensure that institutional actors execute the policies we entrust to them.

Providing we make an adequate investment of civic energy and political commitment as a community, we can devise strategies for monitoring the access of distress migrants to basic social protection, including to adequate nutrition and physical safety, to appropriate schooling, to competent health care. We can also assess distress migrants' access to competent legal representation; we can investigate resettlement figures against quotas promised; we can scrutinize the numbers of grants of asylum or international scholarships or infrastructural project investments to gauge institutional performance relevant to our duties to needy strangers.

How obligatory are the "long strand" duties that Shue's image presents? Some have answered this question by defining our duties to strangers more narrowly than Shue does – shifting the terrain from the somewhat elastic scope of our potential impact to our human need for membership within a circumscribed community. The prime determinants of our hospitality obligations to others, then, with limited exceptions, are the views of those within a community of common values. Michael Walzer, an influential political theorist, has argued that the primary good that we distribute to one another is membership in our collectivity, our country, a bounded community of shared meanings and ways of life (whatever they may be). As its members, we are entitled to preserve the community by shaping it according to our preferences, including by regulating the entry of strangers. We regulate their entry on the basis of our shared understandings of what is just, understandings that are a historical product of debate and collective agreement within our collectivity. Walzer draws a thought-provoking analogy: "Affluent and free countries are, like elite universities, besieged by applicants. They have to decide on their own size and character. . . . [A]s citizens of such a country, we have to decide: Whom should we admit?"[10]

But elite universities are not democratic polities, and university admission criteria are institutional decisions, not open to public scrutiny or revision. Affluent and free countries, by contrast, are riven with contestation and public discussion about admission criteria, in part because the polities themselves are increasingly diverse. As a result, a shared moral universe is elusive as a basis for determining membership. To address this difficulty, some philosophers have resorted to principles of rationality as a basis for delimiting our duties to others.

According to Immanuel Kant, hospitality is a right that belongs to all human beings, because they are all members of a world republic, a "cosmopolis," where they may come into contact with each other, for example at the borders of states. "They have . . . [this right of hospitality] by virtue of their common possession of the surface of the earth, where, as a globe, they cannot infinitely disperse and hence must finally tolerate the presence of each other."[11] In Kant's account, this right of hospitality is not culturally or historically specific, but rather it is a universal obligation tied to our common humanity.

Some have taken this Kantian notion of a shared human destiny to stress the moral irrelevance of the privileges that come from one's place of birth and to justify an ethical obligation to enact generous immigration policies. The Canadian political theorist Joseph Carens argues that free intra-state migration is ethically no different from inter-state free movement, as an instrumental and intrinsic good: "The radical disjuncture that treats freedom of movement within the state as a human right while granting states discretionary control over freedom of movement across state borders makes no moral sense."[12] For Carens, state boundaries are merely "assumptive propositions," neither natural nor inevitable. It follows, for him, that there needs to be some compelling rational justification for immigration measures that cause or perpetuate human suffering: compelling national security exigencies might be one such justification. He argues that a just global policy should reduce inter-state inequality so that migration becomes less essential as a strategy to fulfill people's basic needs, a point I agree with and return to in Chapter 4.

So far, I have considered work focused on the hospitality and solidarity duties generated by religious faiths and rational reflection – our acceptance of our common humanity (Kant), our ability to affect change (Shue), our collective agreements delineating membership (Walzer). All these ethical strands have influenced the protections delivered by state membership and international norms. But, as the Kurdi incident demonstrated, a powerful image of a complete stranger can elicit an intense emotional response that redirects policy within days. There is an unseemly, some would say even pornographic, aspect to these manipulative images, because (without any permission from those represented) they exploit the intense suffering of the vulnerable to elicit knee-jerk short-term do-gooding instead of a more sustained engagement with underlying political challenges. On the other hand, these humanitarian narratives provide the impetus for interrupting the political status quo: "ameliorative action is represented as possible, effective and therefore morally imperative."[13]

Our sense of duty is a syncretic product of religious tradition, rational reflection, and emotion

– emotion that, as the French social scientist Didier Fassin notes, viscerally connects us to the situation of "others," even if they are distant. This visceral connection may be a consequence of our common heritage, or our increasingly shared communications universe. Israeli legal scholar Itamar Mann calls the outcome generated by this process of identification, the "rights of encounter." He argues that when we confront a situation where we are responsible (in however direct or mediated a way) for the life or death of another human being, we face "a command of conscience triggered by defenseless human presence."[14] Reason and emotion combine to create in us, individually and collectively, the experience of an imperative: to act, to save, to help, to share. The Kurdi case bears out what Fassin and Mann argue.

Our Common Humanity

As our current political context makes all too evident, not all individuals or collectivities confronted by the evidence of others' desperation experience a humanitarian imperative. Suspicion, fear, and anxious attachment to traditional customs generate powerful and countervailing demands to the expansive engagement with the needs of others, including support for border closure and opposition to humanitarian aid.

Drawing on the evidence of the Holocaust and its aftermath for millions of displaced and stateless people in mid-20th-century Europe, the illustrious political scientist Hannah Arendt forcefully pointed out the terrifying vulnerability of people forced to rely on international protection. Without access to the support of a state, she argued, human beings are reduced to a state of nature. They are like King Lear, wandering unhinged in the storm without kingdom or family. The protections we have put in place in the half-century since Arendt wrote have progressively lost their efficacy. The massive loss of life in the Mediterranean these past few years, the despair facing Syrian, Afghan, and, now, a new generation of South Sudanese refugees, together with the huge and protracted refugee camp population, demonstrate just how ineffective our enacted obligations to needy strangers are in practice.

The imperatives that stem from our common humanity will persist. Because we share not only the surface of the earth but a common, deeply intertwined set of interests and an ultimate dependence on each other, the duties we owe strangers have to be capacious, clear, and sustainable. The next chapter examines whether our current legislative apparatus achieves this set of ambitious goals.

3

The System at Breaking Point

Prominent public figures from opposite points of the political spectrum have for some time pronounced our systems for managing migration flows terminally broken. For President Obama, this was self-evident: "Today, our immigration system is broken – and everybody knows it."[1] Geert Wilders, a far right politician in the Netherlands, concurred: "Take a walk down the street and see how things are going. You no longer feel you are living in your own country. . . . A country without a border is like a person in a house without a front door. Anybody can enter and you cannot ask anybody to leave. So it's not a real country at all."[2] Critics point to a diverse array of debilitating symptoms, among which ineffective national border control is widely considered the most significant. But, the dramatic loss of life and the dire humanitarian circumstances of refugees and other distress migrants are also symptoms of a system not fit for purpose.

The obsession with the failure of our refugee and migration systems extends beyond politicians, to include artists. Apart from the news media, a thriving industry of cultural products captures the border-crossing breakdown and its human fallout. The 2017 Academy Awards included two Oscar-nominated documentaries about the refugee crisis – *Fire at Sea* and *4.1 Miles*. *Exit West*, a highly acclaimed fictional love story about two refugees, by Mohsin Hamid, author of *The Reluctant Fundamentalist*, was on the bestseller list for weeks. Several hit songs and high profile art exhibitions also address migration topics. A powerful sense of collective dismay and impotence in the face of rising xenophobia and migrant despair is now also a regular feature of glossy weekend magazine special issues. Beyond dismay or despair, is there room for an alternative view? Is there a way to fix this situation?

Mobility and Immobility: A Humanitarian not a Migration Crisis

With all this doom-laden consensus, it might come as something of a surprise to learn that for millions, border crossing at an unprecedentedly brisk rate proceeds perfectly smoothly. According to the UN World Tourism Organization, there were more than 1,000 million international tourists in 2016, a 3.9 percent increase from 2015. In the US alone, 390 million people entered the country in 2016, while 620 million international tourists entered the EU in 2016, and more than 40 million people arrived in Australia. More than 15 million Schengen visas, entry permissions for travelers not entitled to visa-free access to the EU, were issued that year. Apart from short-term travelers, other types of mobility are also at very high levels. For example, the US had more than 1 million international students studying in the country during the 2015/16 academic year; Australia issued more than 200,000 work visas during the same period.

We take this aspect of the global migration system for granted. We talk about a system in crisis, but ignore the fact that a very large part of the system is working just fine. Most travelers are unlikely to encounter evidence of administrative malfunction – their mobility is safe, legal, and regular. The boundaries of this mobility are defined, primarily and variously, by states themselves, though human rights and regional obligations also play a role in establishing permissible exclusion parameters. States amend their laws to adjust the balance between facilitating mobility and protecting domestic assets as they see fit, "in order to make . . . [their] own favorite experiments toward the ideal social republic of the future," as John Maynard Keynes said in 1933.[3] The abrupt 2016 change in migration policy by Sweden, one of the most generous refugee hosting states in the recent period, illustrates this sort of adjustment. Despite a long-standing commitment to promoting refugee family reunification, in the face of the large increase in refugee arrivals over the previous 18 months, the Swedish government abruptly decided to bar further family-based entry for refugees.

Though the current system works smoothly for some refugees and migrants, this is not the case overall. In particular, many who desperately need access to migration are excluded from legal and safe mobility options. As a result, what we have is not so much a migration as a humanitarian or reception crisis. The migration system is not working because it fails to deliver any legitimate or safe exit strategy from deeply distressing, often untenable circumstances – life-threatening conflict, indefinite economic misery, devastating climate change, lack of opportunity, persistent exposure to violence. Those excluded from entry or deported post entry are typically victims of a system of radical global inequality that impinges most dramatically on populations that are poor and nonwhite. This system has generated some fairly disastrous human consequences, one of which is the very large-scale distress migration we are witnessing.

Several aspects of this serious systemic breakdown are noteworthy. One is the length of time millions face in supposedly "temporary" situations – the average length of time spent in a refugee camp is now 10 years, an indictment of the encampment approach to protection and of humanitarianism more broadly. For many populations, including Palestinians, Somalis, and Rohingya, a third generation is eking out a painful and minimal existence in camps, a "zone of exclusion" beyond the bounds of ordinary social intercourse.

Another symptom of systemic failure is the maldistribution of hosting responsibility. More than 86 percent of refugees live in the developing world, many marooned in some of its poorest countries, often in inhospitable – arid and isolated – areas, a situation that militates against the possibility of self-sufficiency, of reconstructing a productive and fulfilling life.

Perhaps most egregious of all is the growing sense that millions of distress migrants have no legal or safe exit strategy available to them because they do not meet the criteria for an award of refugee status or for any other legal immigration category. The choice then is entrapment in unlivable situations or hazardous, even life-threatening, hope-fueled migration toward an uncertain future plagued by the burden of irregular migration status, with the ever present risk of deportation and exploitation that accompanies that status.

These three major deficiencies and ways to address them will be discussed in more detail in Chapter 4.

Distress Migration

I call the element of migration flows that creates the sense of crisis "distress migration." This is migration that generates a crisis mentality because it is largely uncontrolled by states and, in significant measure, is not legally authorized. It is migration that stems from desperation, vulnerability, and need, from living circumstances that are experienced as unbearable or deeply unsatisfactory and that precipitate serious obstacles to a reasonable or tolerable life. It is migration that, years after the decision to leave home, may continue to expose people to the risk of irregular status, and with it to a lack of identity documents or of entitlement to work, attend school, or secure health care.

In my conception, distress migration encompasses – but is broader than – several other terms commonly used to describe "forced migration," such as refugee flight or survival migration. Refugee flight covers situations where people are forced to flee from their country for fear of persecution as a result of their civil or political status – because of their religion, their race, their political opinion, or their nationality for example. It does not cover people fleeing general political instability or state failure. The international definition of a refugee is set out in the UN Convention on the Status of Refugees, and that definition has been widely incorporated into domestic legal regimes.[4] Qualifying as a refugee gives a distress migrant a substantial advantage over other migrants, because refugee status protects the person from being sent back to the place they have fled from. Syrians fleeing persecution by the Assad regime are likely to qualify as refugees and to receive a legal status in the first host country they flee to if they make an asylum (synonymous with refugee) application. By contrast, Libyans, Somalis, Afghans, Hondurans, or Pakistanis who migrate because of political instability and state failure are unlikely to qualify as refugees or to be allowed to remain. This difference in protection outcomes explains why Syrian passports have become a much sought-after commodity for would-be migrants, trading for 30 times more at the end of 2016 than they were two years earlier ($7,000 compared to $250). If a Libyan can pass as a Syrian, he or she is much more likely to be able to remain abroad.

Survival migration is a somewhat broader concept, advanced by the British social scientist Alexander Betts. The concept covers people outside their country of origin because of an existential threat for which no domestic remedy is available.[5] The existential threat may be political (as is the case for refugees), but it may also be the result of other causes – climate change or state failure for example. If survival migration were accepted as a basis for affording legal protection (which is not the case at the moment), it would place the Libyan in the above example in the same position as the Syrian. It would also afford protection to people fleeing natural disasters such as devastating hurricanes or earthquakes.

Neither refugee flight nor survival migration, as defined, covers the circumstances of millions leaving home to escape chronic destitution or hopelessness. These are distress migrants who feel that mobility presents the only viable exit option from a life of endless scarcity, suffering, and lack of opportunity. They are people who could survive at home, people who do not face persecution or existential threats but who would not enjoy fundamental elements of a rights respecting life, including the hope of fulfilling basic aspirations. In my view, these migrants should be entitled to exercise mobility as a matter of fundamental justice, as one strategy (among others) for reducing global inequality. The term "distress migration" covers the African teenager facing a life of unemployment and penury, anxious to secure an education that delivers the possibility of a good job; it covers the Central American woman desperate to leave a gang-infested neighborhood with her small children before they are recruited or killed; it covers the Afghan youth charged with finding resources to support a widowed mother and younger siblings forced back to a war-torn country; it covers adolescents from Morocco, Eritrea, Pakistan, and Colombia abandoning dead-end situations in search of a future. To encompass these populations, distress migration is a necessary addition to our lexicon.

To address how we can fix the refugee and migration crisis, we need to understand the basic building blocks of the system that regulates border control internationally as a whole. We can then identify the sources of key problems and possible solutions.

Crossing Borders: The Building Blocks of Modern International Mobility and Immigration Control

As we saw in Chapter 1, every group and every generation faces the question of whether to move and if so who among its members to select for migration. These constraints, however, do not concern us here. What is at issue is the migration management system operated by states that enables effortless border crossing for some, but generates insuperable obstacles for others.

Until the late 19th century, enforced restrictions on human movement were largely the work of private actors, such as feudal lords or slave owners, who targeted fellow inhabitants of their lands rather than outsiders. No state legislated immigration control measures to regulate the entry of non-citizens. Indeed, as noted in Chapter 1, by far the largest abuse in matters of human migration was not forced exclusion or removal from national territory but rather the forced importation of enslaved or indentured populations. Between 1500 and 1875, the US imported more than 300,000 slaves and Great Britain traded more than 3 million slaves.

General mobility increased considerably over the course of the 19th century as feudalism gave way to economic liberalism and the unshackling of the laboring classes. The support of free movement of people and goods across state borders is well captured by the 1889 International Emigration Conference resolution: "We affirm the right of the individual to come and go and dispose of his person and his destinies as he pleases."[6]

All this changed as hostility toward foreigners, particularly those clearly identifiable as "other," increased with rising nationalism and the widespread diffusion of the notions of racial superiority, inferiority, and purity discussed in Chapter 1. Even though global measures to attract skilled immigrants made economic sense (still today, in several major destination states, including the US, immigrants pay more in taxes than they cost the state in public services, and employer organizations strongly favor immigration), nativism began to prevail. Half a century after the US and then UK introduced immigration control laws restricting population entry on the basis of race, Australia's "White Australia" policy adopted a similar approach, to avoid "being swamped by the rush of peoples from the over-crowded countries of the world," a reference of course to the "teeming millions" of Asians, not immigrants from the over-crowded UK.[7] In all these countries, these early border control measures seeded later restrictive laws progressively targeting larger and larger constituencies of potential entrants and eventually subjecting all those who were not citizens, permanent residents, or other carefully defined exempt groups to immigration control. To this day, with the exception of some frontiers within free movement areas such as parts of the EU and the Mercosur Latin American region, legal border crossing requires production of proof of identity and eligibility to enter by everyone. A central building block of our current migration control system, then, is general acceptance of the legitimacy of scrutiny of individuals as they enter state territory.

A precondition for the implementation of comprehensive border control is the development of an unequivocal means to identify each entrant, a second building block and a development that presupposed an effective bureaucracy able to scrutinize proof of identity. With the transition from feudalism, principalities, and small city states to the development of national states, boundary control moved from the perimeters of municipalities to the confines of states, from local to national control.

In step with this transition went the creation of portable tools – identity documents, passports – that replicated in mobile form the information long stored about individuals in municipal registries. These tools for unique identification enabled states to clearly identify their citizens and, eventually, to distinguish between different categories of border crosser and their eligibility for entry. Together, these two building blocks of our current system of migration management, an insistence on the legitimacy of border control and the ability to uniquely identify individuals presenting themselves at a border by national status and other attributes relevant to admissibility, remain fundamental elements in the administration of immigration control.

As the destination of choice for very large numbers of would-be immigrants from across the globe, the US was a forerunner in the use of both building blocks as it developed its system of national immigration control. In 1856, reversing the previous primacy of individual states to determine immigration laws and issue US passports, the US Congress asserted the federal government's exclusive right to control both. This process set in train a series of developments similar to those that occurred within the EU over a century later – freedom of movement within the territory for citizens from different states, but rigorous border control at the external periphery.

Between the 1880s and the 1910s, other Western countries, including France, Germany, and the UK, also moved toward restrictive foreigner control immigration regimes that required would-be entrants to produce their national passports as a precondition to admission. The building blocks of the contemporary migration management system had been set. Within less than half a century, a celebration of the benefits of free movement had been replaced by suspicion of foreign entrants and the requirement that those with a claim to legal entry – whether temporarily or permanently – prove their bona fides.

The framework of immigration control today
While citizens do not need a visa or any special permission to enter their own countries (a valid national passport is sufficient), non-citizens require legal authority to enter, whether on a temporary or a permanent basis. Travel might be motivated by multiple reasons (work and study, family reunification and business), but permission to enter is based on the primary motive for migrating. Though each country has its own precise immigration categories and qualifying conditions attached to them, there

are four broad types of migration situation, excluding refugee or humanitarian categories, that cover non-citizens who do not already have permanent residence: travel for work, travel for family reunification, travel to visit, and travel for study. In addition, some countries, such as the US, also have "diversity" immigration, an annual lottery-based system for a limited number of immigrants not otherwise eligible. Within these broad categories, many subdivisions exist.

Within the travel for work category are people with work permits (sometimes, but not always, allowed to bring dependents with them and to extend their visas) and people on particular short-term agricultural or other "guest worker" contracts (usually not allowed to bring dependents or to extend their visas). Within the travel for family reunification category are spouses and minor children left behind in the home country when a family member first migrated to seek work, elderly parents dependent on a child who left home to seek their fortune decades earlier, and fiancés joining future spouses. Visitors may be tourists, entrepreneurs exploring business opportunities, relatives maintaining contact with family members, members of sports teams or performing groups.

There are some overarching distinctions that cut

across immigration category. Some migrants travel on temporary visas, some arrive for settlement as permanent residents (often sponsored by family members); some benefit from visa-free travel (preferential status given to nationals of some countries), some have to obtain a visa from the destination country consulate before traveling. In the latter case, immigration control takes place in more than one site – at the consular office abroad first, and then at the port of entry. In some cases, passengers also require transit visas to facilitate their movement en route.

States categorize migrants and their entry eligibility depending on their countries of origin, and often apply different criteria even within nationality categories, depending on the migrants' economic status, race, gender, or age. A system of extensive official discretion, at the consular offices abroad, at the port of entry, and at post-entry immigration centers, complicates the migration process in practice. As a result, whereas some categories of passengers can rely on sailing through immigration unhindered on each occasion, others can expect probing questions, and sometimes hostile and prolonged interviews that may result in detention pending a decision or in outright refusal of permission to enter a country. As a general rule, affluent, educated, and skilled applicants (particularly those who are Caucasian), especially if they are legally represented, have little difficulty navigating this system and securing legal entry. At varying historical moments, in response to domestic labor force needs, unskilled or semi-skilled migrants, often from former colonies, have also enjoyed streamlined immigration procedures.

Migration that takes place outside this system of controls is, by definition, irregular. People who enter without presenting themselves to an immigration officer (clandestine entry), people who enter with false documents or on the basis of false statements, or people who enter legally but then overstay the length of their temporary permission are all considered irregular. Regrettably, they are routinely referred to as "illegals" or by other derogatory terms such as "bogus refugees," as if the person rather than his or her legal status were flawed. Irregular migrants are increasingly treated as criminals, charged with immigration offences and imprisoned, a process that aggravates vulnerability and misery.

Paper proof of eligibility for entering a country – passports with photographs and visa stamps, sometimes supplemented by birth, marriage, adoption, death, or doctors' certificates, employers' job offer letters, educational qualifications, bank account statements, relatives' invitation letters – is increasingly supplemented by more invasive evidentiary requirements for determining identity. These include DNA tests, first used in the 1980s, data on criminal and migration history stored in national, regional, or international databases, and, more recently, biometric tools such as iris scans and fingerprints. This proliferating archive of data has rendered the passport itself the tip of a cyber surveillance iceberg, that can probe not only the body but also the behavior, social and economic standing, and political connections of the would-be entrant.

An exception to this regime of border control and identity verification are free movement zones in some regions of the world. Mercosur covers Latin America, the Nordic Common Labour Market applies to the Scandinavian countries, and there are common markets in Central Africa, West Africa, and the Trans-Tasman Travel arrangement between Australia and New Zealand. In these areas, member states of the area or zone agree to remove internal border controls so that goods, services, capital, and also people (citizens of the states and their families) can move freely within the zone. The most powerful of these entities is the EU, the largest economic trading bloc in the world. Although each EU member state applies its own domestic laws to the regulation of immigration for migrants arriving from outside the bloc (so-called third country nationals), all member states are required to allow citizens from any EU member state (and their families) to enter, work, and settle.

This freedom of movement for EU nationals has had a transformational impact on the continent. It has contributed to reducing regional disparities and raising collective standards of living, facilitating economic opportunity, and stimulating cultural exchange.

Another aspect of the free movement of persons within the EU is the elimination of internal borders between EU member states. Once a person has been allowed to enter the EU, he or she can move freely within the whole free movement (so-called Schengen) zone. Even non-EU citizens with a limited-term "Schengen visa" can enter via any external border and travel within the EU for the duration of that visa without again having to show a passport. Not all EU member states opted into the free movement zone. Even before Brexit, the UK, for example, maintained its borders (though it has operated a Common Travel Area with Ireland). Within Schengen-land, however, there were, until the erection of barriers by Hungary, Bulgaria, and Greece in response to the migration "crisis" in

2015, no borders. The vision of a border-free zone of peace and prosperity, where conflict and division had for so long been the norm, has been inspiring and beneficial to the European continent as a whole, a model for other regions.

Fleeing Persecution: A Legitimate Claim on Hospitality?

Though the entry of non-citizens is always subject to control at the external border of a country (or free travel area), one group of migrants has maintained a privileged status, at least as a matter of international law and public policy – namely, refugees. Unlike the migration system, which, as we have just seen, is governed by domestic laws and domestic institutions (though regional free movement areas have partially qualified this national monopoly), the modern refugee system has been more closely governed by international obligations.

The modern refugee protection system originates in the period surrounding World War II, though decades earlier, Minorities Treaties were created to address the very sizeable numbers of refugees fleeing persecution and pogroms in the aftermath of the Armenian genocide, the Russian Revolution, and the devastation caused by World War I across Europe. The first institution specifically established for refugees was the United Nations Relief and Rehabilitation Administration (UNRRA), created by allied leaders during World War II to provide material assistance to refugees and to help them return home. Though many of the displaced did return home (UNRRA repatriated 7 million people in just four months in 1945), others were unable or unwilling to return to their former countries in Eastern Europe, a trend still highly evident today. By 1946 well over a million displaced persons were still languishing in Allied camps, with the US's decision (fueled by an active Jewish lobby) to resettle approximately 5,000 among this population, hardly making a dent. It took another two years for the US to respond more generously. The result was a 1948 Displaced Persons Act, the first piece of national legislation to recognize what has become a permanent aspect of contemporary migration management: the distinction between immigrants and refugees.

After World War II a new institution was established, this time by the United Nations – the International Refugee Organization. Its mandate was to facilitate the resettlement of refugees who were unable or unwilling to return to their home countries. But, like UNRRA, this organization did not survive long. It was replaced, in 1951, by the United Nations High Commissioner for Refugees (UNHCR), an entity that continues to this day, now much expanded in scope, personnel, and influence. In tandem with the creation of this refugee protection organization, the international community also established a legal instrument that was to have enduring effect, the 1951 UN Convention on the Status of Refugees. This Convention, and the 1967 Protocol to it that expanded the Convention's applicability beyond the displacements of World War II, are, together with UNHCR, central elements of the contemporary refugee system.

One of the signature achievements of the UN Refugee Convention is the establishment of a widely adopted legal regime that prohibits the return, or "*refoulement*," of a refugee to a country where his or her life or freedom would be threatened. This *non refoulement* obligation has enabled millions fleeing persecution to find safe alternative homes and a permanent legal status outside their country of origin.

Another important outcome of the Convention is a legal definition of refugee that is internationally accepted. The 145 states that have ratified the convention operate with a common standard, and this facilitates cooperation and some collaboration in the management of refugee cases.

Broadly speaking there are two ways in which refugees get legal residence in Western countries. One is through the overseas refugee resettlement program, which brings in from abroad people already recognized by UNCHR as refugees according to the Convention definition. Countries such as the US, Canada, Australia, France, Hungary, and the UK all operate overseas refugee resettlement programs, admitting a nationally set annual quota of these so-called "Convention refugees." The other way refugees gain legal status is by making a successful refugee (or asylum) application at the port of entry of a country outside their own. This is the procedure used by people who need the protection of the state they are in (or want to enter), but who are not yet classified as refugees.

Both procedures are, in practice, fraught with difficulty. In the case of the overseas refugee resettlement program, the resettlement rate is vastly inadequate to the demand, so that only a fraction of the 21 million global refugees have any prospects of benefiting. This explains the dramatic rise in the numbers of so-called "protracted" refugees, trapped in a situation that the philosopher Giorgio Agamben has referred to as a "zone of exception."[8]

The limited availability of resettlement slots is compounded by increasingly harsh security screening procedures, by restrictive family unity rules (forcing people to separate from relatives they consider members of their immediate family), and in some cases by onerous sponsorship requirements. The result is years, sometimes decades, of debilitating limbo for refugees, a situation already mentioned earlier. Palestinians in Gaza and the West Bank have been living in camps for over 60 years. The restrictions and despair engendered by camps have led many, the majority of refugees globally, to elect for life outside refugee camps. Though Zaatari, the sprawling Syrian refugee camp in Jordan, is now that country's second largest "city" with an estimated population of some 79,000, over 90 percent of Syrian refugees live outside camps, in makeshift urban contexts where daily life is harsh and insecure, and access to education and health care is elusive and severely inadequate.

The in-country asylum procedure is also beset with difficulties and uncertainties. Already by the early 2000s, then UK Minister of State for Asylum and Immigration, Lord Rooker, openly agreed that there were no legal avenues through which bona fide asylum seekers could enter the UK.[9] The imposition of visa requirements on nationals from war-torn or unstable countries, of onerous fines on airlines or shipping companies that transport passengers without the required visa, and of draconian interdiction measures blocking sea access to safe ports, have made the process of seeking asylum increasingly dangerous, expensive, and physically and psychologically oppressive.

This is why rates of mortality are high and the use of smugglers is virtually obligatory to reach a border where an asylum application can be made. Even when the border is reached, border officials often refuse entry and send asylum applicants back because they consider them ineligible to have their cases considered. There are many situations where this can happen: the asylum seekers come from a country considered safe, they have passed through a country en route where the officials think they should have made their asylum application (a process that in the EU is governed by the Dublin Convention), they have already applied for asylum elsewhere, their story is not considered credible, they have already been refused asylum in the past. For those asylum seekers lucky enough not to be summarily removed, other challenges often arise. Many are imprisoned while their cases are considered. Lengthy and often hostile questioning to establish eligibility for refugee status follows every asylum application, and, despite the significant legal complexities of the process, access to legal representation and quality interpretation are elusive. For asylum seekers fortunate enough not to be in detention, access to work or welfare benefits while their cases are considered is not assured, so survival itself is a challenge. These extreme hardships of course compound the trauma of exile and loss afflicting distress migrants as they await news of their fate. Small wonder that suicide of asylum seekers is a not infrequent occurrence.

Added to these personal difficulties are the significant legal uncertainties relating to the outcome of the asylum application. Despite the uniform definition of a refugee, decision makers exercise considerable discretion. Furthermore, government policies change, so that asylum seekers who count on the positive experience of relatives or peers who precede them in the quest for protection may face unexpected exclusion. For example, as discussed earlier, young Afghan men fleeing forced conscription by the Taliban are less likely to succeed in their asylum claims now than they were some years ago.

In addition, there is little uniformity in the way different countries interpret the Refugee Convention. The information about levels of risk in refugee-sending countries may vary, and foreign policy considerations may affect the willingness to grant protection in different ways. As a result, asylum applicants often experience very different outcomes to applications based on similar facts. For example, in 2016, Canada reported an 82 percent acceptance rate for refugees from Eritrea, while Israel's acceptance rate was 0.4 percent. Even within countries, enormous discrepancies in refugee acceptance rates exist. In the US, the discrepancy is so large that the system has been called a "refugee roulette," with some decision makers granting more than 90 percent of cases and others less than 10 percent. It follows that predicting the outcome of an asylum case is difficult, and delay and uncertainty create psychologically corrosive hardship.

Despite these severe obstacles and challenges, refugee status remains a precious and critically important humanitarian remedy. Few if any other legal protections have delivered desperately needed safety and rescue from harm, saved lives at risk, and enabled dramatic improvements in survival prospects for millions who would otherwise be trapped in or forced back to murderous states.

The Convention defines a refugee as someone with "a well-founded fear of being persecuted for reasons of race, religion, nationality, membership of a particular social group, or political opinion,

[who] is outside the country of his nationality, and is unable to or, owing to such fear, unwilling to avail himself of the protection of that country."[10] It thus covers people fleeing political persecution (e.g., because they are visible opponents of an authoritarian regime), or religious persecution (e.g., because they belong to a stigmatized and unprotected minority), or persecution on the basis of other personal characteristics such as race or nationality. Over the years, thanks to a complex process of human rights advocacy, test case litigation, and social norm change, the scope of protection of refugees has expanded, although again with considerable national variation. From its original core constituency of visible political dissidents and persecuted religious and national minorities (including Soviet Jews, anti-Shah Iranians and anti-apartheid South Africans, Sri Lankan Tamils, Chilean and Argentinian opponents of dictatorship), some jurisdictions have accepted as Convention refugees people fleeing forced circumcision (also known as female genital mutilation), persecutory homophobia, persistent and severe domestic violence, recruitment as a child soldier, child exploitation, exposure to gang recruitment and trafficking. To jeopardize the continued operation of this system of international legal protection, for example, by

opening up the Convention for renegotiation in the hopes of expanding its protective scope (a strategy sometimes proposed), would be irresponsible.

Urgent and Unfinished Business

For some, the contemporary system of migration and refugee management works well. But for a sizeable number of distress migrants, it constitutes a significant, sometimes impenetrable and brutal obstacle. With some exceptions, such as the voluminous migrant worker schemes in the Gulf States, the international immigration system tends to favor economically and socially privileged adult migrants over those who are poor, young, uneducated, or unskilled, unless the latter have close family ties that enable family-based migration. The refugee system is based on an individualized decision making system that caters to those fleeing state (and limited other) persecution, but excludes many other distress migrants who fall outside the scope of the Convention. This large population – of failed asylum seekers, of over-stayers, of irregular migrants, of deportees, of internally and otherwise displaced persons, and of exploited children on the move – is the source of our current preoccupation with a migration and refugee system not fit for purpose. How can we more adequately address the urgent and compelling needs of these populations? This is a question we will turn to in the next chapter.

4

Finding Workable and Humane Solutions

Albeit not at the rate of the 2015/16 Mediterranean exodus, people still continue to cram into dinghies, to pay vast amounts to smugglers, and to die in search of safety. In the first half of 2017, as I write, more than 100 people a month have drowned in the Mediterranean. Distress migration of South Sudanese fleeing civil war and Central Americans escaping criminal violence also persists at a high rate. What is being done to address these human crises? And what needs to be done to generate sustainable and just solutions?

For the first time in its 70-year history, the UN General Assembly held a plenary summit in September 2016 focused on the issue of migration. Unlike other major international issues, such as global epidemics or trade or international crime, migration had never before been the subject of a plan to generate international cooperation between UN member states. Powerful incentives are necessary to stimulate a willingness to reach agreement on this polarizing issue. But these incentives there now are. Europe had not witnessed anything on the scale, or with the political impact, of the 2015 population arrivals for over seven decades. This final chapter considers the issues that are most central to resolving the refugee and migration crisis, some of the measures undertaken so far, and additional strategies needed to generate sustainable and just outcomes for the future.

Addressing Some Key Drivers of Distress Migration

Most of the attention dedicated to fixing the refugee and migration crisis has been directed to epiphenomena, symptoms of what is not working, rather than to the underlying drivers. The focus has been on failing border control, on over-crowded refugee camps, on smuggler fees, on trafficker exploitation, on the challenges of resettlement and integration. These symptoms certainly need attention, not only because of the human distress they generate, but also because of their spillover effects, both fiscally and politically.

Finding Workable and Humane Solutions

Ultimately, however, searching for solutions to the refugee and migration crisis by focusing on epiphenomena is a futile project, doomed to failure. Distress migration flows cannot be stopped merely by ever more vigorous border control, humanitarian aid, or prosecution of smugglers. The more resilient, healthy, and capable migrants carve out their own alternatives. The smuggler price for a Syrian family of four to get from Libya to Northern Europe has mushroomed to about $36,000, a tariff that reflects not only the desperation to flee but also the inflation caused by generous contributions of the Syrian diaspora. Central Americans fleeing gang violence are ensnared by criminal networks that provide cross-border transport in return for drug smuggling or sexual favors. Afghans and Sudanese make repeated attempts to cross at great personal risk and psychological cost, until they are successful. If they are blocked in transit states, they do what it takes to move on – often engaging in risky and exploitative activities to raise the fees for smugglers. The less resilient and vigorous, more than 20 million to date, languish for years or decades in depressing and dead-end situations, in camps or urban centers, hoping for resettlement. They may be out of sight for Western publics, but this outcome does not constitute a sustainable or just solution.

Finding Workable and Humane Solutions

Addressing symptoms then, important and necessary though that is, is neither a comprehensive nor a rational strategy. To generate sustainable solutions, we need to probe the drivers of contemporary distress migration. No easy or rapid solutions will emerge. Instead, I hope to offer a convincing account of the key underlying issues that need to be seriously tackled in addition to the narrow migration management symptoms already touched on.

Conflict

One of the most significant and obvious drivers of distress migration is conflict.[1] No amount of managed migration or economic development will prevent outflows of refugees intent on saving their lives.

The extent of conflict has varied, even within the relatively recent past. According to the Center for Systemic Peace, while global conflict decreased by 60 percent between 1991 and the early 2000s, the trend has since been reversing. The Peace Research Institute in Oslo reports that the number of armed conflicts rose from 41 in 2014 to 50 in 2015, and that the trend is upwards.[2]

Many wars last for long periods of time,

exacerbating the impact on affected populations and the size of population outflows, and reducing the chances of voluntary repatriation. In 2014, the average length of exile for refugees from 33 countries affected by conflict was 25 years.[3] The six-year conflict in Syria has led to the displacement of over half the country's 22 million population and more than 4 million refugees, destabilizing the whole region, with spillover effects much further afield. The 2013 outbreak of civil war in South Sudan has also led to massive displacement. By January 2017, more than 1.2 million South Sudanese had fled to Uganda, Ethiopia, and other neighboring areas.

Of the refugees and migrants fleeing to Europe in 2016, almost 60 percent have come from the world's top 10 refugee-producing countries, all affected by conflict. The burden of this massive cost of war is very unequally distributed – only seven countries, all of them outside the Global North, host over 50 percent of the world's refugees. This explains why it took the 2015/16 Mediterranean refugee and migration "crisis" to trigger serious international attention to the issue.

Reducing conflict is therefore at the top of the list for long-term solutions to the refugee and migration crisis. A detailed examination of the tools available to reduce global conflict is beyond the scope of this book. And indeed conflict resolution is one of the most complex global challenges in its own right. It is clear, however, that new data mining resources, including geospatial crisis mapping and crowd sourcing, enhance our collective capabilities to develop early warning systems designed to prevent atrocities and reduce the risk of conflict in the first place. Attention to changing patterns showing increases in hate speech, in xenophobic legislation, in population flows, and in violence targeted at particular minorities can trigger warnings. These warnings can and should stimulate vigorous preventive diplomatic measures to avert outright conflict and the mass population flows that they trigger. Rwanda, Bosnia, Syria, and South Sudan stand as stark reminders of the cost of inaction on evident but ignored warning signs.

In addition to data mining, more traditional tools for reducing or averting conflict are also key. There is a voluminous literature on the use of smart and other sanctions, as well as a plethora of international or regional mechanisms, to avert hot war. Curbing weapon proliferation and the legitimacy of a flourishing transnational arms industry, supported by the major global players who are key arms suppliers, is another important strategy. The sale of arms to dictatorial regimes is a key driver of contemporary conflict and thus of large-scale distress migration.

There is also a growing body of evidence showing that outside military interventions to remove dictatorial and authoritarian regimes rarely produce democratic substitutes or an end to conflict, unless they complement leadership from well-organized and strong opposition forces within the affected society. Military intervention can have extremely negative consequences, not least of which is the inevitable knock-on effect into massive population displacement far beyond the immediate territory. Recent experience in Afghanistan, Iraq, and Syria bears this out.

In the face of an unstable multipolar world order with several inexperienced and unpredictable political leaders at the helm of some key global players, the challenge of reducing conflict is enormous. But without success on that front, sustainable and significant solutions to distress migration remain elusive. If we do not reduce global conflict and responsibly nurture all avenues for advancing peaceful conflict resolution, the chances of completely solving the migration and refugee crisis anytime soon are nil.

Humanitarian Disasters and Climate Change

Closely related to the distress migration consequences of conflict are those that stem from environmental harms, both natural and man-made. This too is a very large topic that merits a discussion well beyond that offered here. The rate of natural disasters is increasing (three times as many between 2000 and 2009 as there were between 1980 and 1989) with nearly 80 percent of the increase a result of climate-related events. With approximately 200 million people affected each year, the spillover effects on distress migration, particularly internal displacement but international movement too, are immense.

As already noted, these drivers of displacement are not covered by the 1951 Refugee Convention, since those fleeing do not typically have a well-founded fear of persecution because of their civil or political status. Rather, they are caught up in large-scale events that disrupt daily life – earthquakes, extreme precipitation, tsunamis and other strong wind and water storms, or less instantaneous but equally devastating natural events related to climate change, such as sea level rise, deforestation, land and water and air degradation, and desertification.

Man-made hazards also contribute to environmental displacement. Large-scale flooding of agricultural land by massive national dam projects and the replacement of traditional agriculture by huge agribusiness conglomerates have displaced very large populations over decades. Changing demand for traditional cash crops as consumption patterns shift, together with reduced day labor income due to increased agricultural mechanization, play a part in driving urbanization, which in turn is often followed by international distress migration. Moreover, harsh environmental conditions, unpredictable rainfall, and the need to reduce economic risk by diversifying one's income source can combine with other factors including, more generally, poor economic outlooks as a political "threat multiplier," tipping the balance in favor of migration. Migration in turn can lead to conflict and further migration. The situation in Syria exemplifies these complex and interconnected pro-cesses. Changing agricultural production patterns together with a dramatic decline in rainfall in Eastern Syria over years – and particularly in the four-year period before the outbreak of war – precipitated the westward flow of large numbers of Sunni peasants, raising interethnic tensions and contributing to the outbreak of war.

The scale of disaster- and climate-related migra-tion is uncertain and a source of some controversy. Since the term "environmental refugees" first emerged in the 1980s, many commentators assert that climate-related migration will dwarf the size of refugee flows today. A commonly cited estimate is that of Norman Myers who, in 2002, predicted more than 200 million climate-induced refugees by 2050; more conservatively, the UN Environmental Program estimates there will be 50 million climate-related refugees by 2060.

Regardless of the variability of total estimates, there is little doubt that environmental factors will increasingly contribute to population displacement even if other drivers interact with them. Noting this, the 2015 Paris Agreement under the UN Framework Convention on Climate Change called for the establishment of a task force to find ways of tackling climate-induced displacement. International collaboration, including on the development of equitable and consensus resettlement and compensation plans, seems an urgent necessity. Deft political leadership and compromise will be essential to progress in this area.

When whole populations are affected by civil unrest and natural calamity, the UN Refugee Convention does not afford a remedy; in such cases, affected populations can sometimes rely on more generous regional conventions, which offer protection to a broader subset of distress migrants. Both Africa and Latin America have promulgated treaties (the 1969 Organization of African Unity Convention Governing the Specific Aspects of Refugee Problems in Africa and the 1984 Cartagena Declaration on Refugees, respectively) that afford protection to people forced to flee their homes because of generalized violence or instability and the serious threats they pose to people's lives and freedom.

However, millions in need of protection are not covered either by the Refugee Convention or by these regional instruments, so their chances of securing a legal migration status when they flee are small. Some benefit from temporary and discretionary schemes set up to alleviate humanitarian suffering after major disasters. An example is the US government's grant in 1998 of temporary protected status to large numbers of Hondurans affected by Hurricane Mitch, the deadliest Atlantic hurricane since 1780, which devastated the lives of more than 1.5 million people. That protection still covers 57,000 Hondurans in the US. The EU has also made extensive use of forms of temporary or humanitarian protection to cover distress migrants who fall outside the scope of refugee protection, starting with the former Yugoslav refugees mentioned in Chapter 1.

Populations, forced out by more gradual and

incremental calamities such as rising sea levels and desertification, have yet to receive comparable treatment. But their needs will become increasingly pressing. Some schemes, such as the Nansen Initiative for migrants affected by climate change, have established disaster preparedness programs to confront migration pressures, alongside the more proximal issues of health care, shelter, and child protection that disasters generate and that will arise with increasing frequency. But this preventive work is in its infancy and needs much greater political and fiscal support to generate effective and protective solutions.

Global Inequality and Poverty

According to British development economist Paul Collier, "mass international migration is a response to extreme global inequality."[4] While this simplistic statement does not explain the forced migration of millions of refugees who only leave home to avoid violence or other forms of persecution, it is clear that global inequality contributes significantly to the pressure to migrate. Much of the inequality-driven migration is regular and legally sanctioned labor migration covered by bilateral or regional labor mobility schemes. The very large-scale migration of South and East Asian workers to the Gulf states is an example. As already noted, this is not the migration that generates a sense of crisis. On the contrary: it has enabled massive wealth expansion for some employers (the beneficiaries of very advantageous tax regimes in the Gulf states) and much needed, even if low, income for large numbers of migrant workers.

Another qualification to Collier's claim is also worth noting. For all its visibility and scale, migration remains the exception rather than the rule in human behavior; only 3 percent of the world's population has migrated internationally. And amongst those who do, it is not generally the poorest who move across borders. Because of the significant costs imposed by international migration, extremely poor and highly stigmatized populations rarely have the resources needed to exercise international mobility. The most disadvantaged members of poor communities, including the disabled (approximately 10 percent of the population), or young mothers and widows, are the least likely to leave, stymied by onerous family responsibilities or lack of access to travel funding. The opposite is true of privileged groups: in 2002 30 percent of all highly educated Ghanaians and Sierra Leoneans lived abroad and

75 percent of university-educated Jamaicans live in the US.[5] These groups are overwhelmingly legal residents, and many are now citizens of their host countries.

Economic need and the lack of opportunity for economic advancement are central factors that compound other drivers of distress migration such as political instability, and social and environmental insecurity. Poor and unskilled migrants from the South working in the Global North are likely to earn in a week more than they would have made in a month at home. A World Bank study of migrants from Togo to New Zealand found that the lifetime gain due to migration was at least $237,000, even before allowing for non-monetary benefits such as higher-quality education and health care, and the effects of wealth accumulation. This represented a 216 percent increase in income, an economic impact with dramatic implications not just for the migrants' lifestyle but also for the standard of living available to their non-migrating families.[6] In 2014, migrants from developing countries sent home an estimated $436 billion in remittances, a figure that dwarfs official development assistance.[7] Thanks to the proliferation of social media and information technology more generally, this vast disparity is more evident than it ever was, particularly to young people.

Finding Workable and Humane Solutions

Distress migration is a response to the lack of economic security, advancement opportunities, and robust social protection back home. These circumstances in turn are a product of drastically unequal trade regimes, and onerous debt servicing agreements that perpetuate vast differences between North and South. The resulting inequalities are exacerbated by development policies that impose harsh fiscal measures, often demanded by international financial institutions, measures that undermine the enjoyment of basic social and economic rights by poor populations. As long as these determinants of global disparities remain unchanged, young people will continue to experience the sense of lack of hope at home and opportunity abroad that renders emigration the default choice for growing numbers, particularly in Africa and Asia.

A failure to address global inequality drives the motivation that fuels mobility. This does not mean that economic development alone will depress migration flows. On the contrary, the American economist David Massey's classic research on Mexico–US flows showed that economic development was actually likely to encourage migration in the short term even though the opposite was more likely in the long term. But programs carefully targeted to alleviate poverty (most effective when benefits are directly placed in the hands of women) can have a significant impact, as research in Mexico on the impact of PROGRESA, the ambitious government poverty alleviation program, shows. By providing conditional cash transfers (funding conditional on performance of desired behavior such as ensuring children's school attendance) to low-income households, the program reduced rural out-migration to international destinations in the short term; however, once rural children received an education, their propensity toward migration increased.[8] Similarly, research in Senegal has found that low-income agrarian households provided with the financial means to diversify their income streams so they could mitigate the risk of crop failure from single crops no longer needed to resort to international migration as a way of insuring against income shocks. Government strategies that sustain livelihoods by promoting safe environments, better yields on agriculture, and diversification of income streams can deflect some of the pressure to migrate.

Stabilizing failing local and state governance structures and countering official corruption are also critically important strategies for reducing the attraction of migration. Where drug lords and gangs terrorize neighborhoods, young people's opportunities to study and find productive work shrink dramatically. An example of the impact of civic intervention to shore up local governance structures is recent US investment in Honduran violence-prevention programs, at an annual cost of approximately $100 million. While this represents a substantial expenditure, it is, as Pulitzer award winner writer Sonia Nazario notes, "pocket change compared with the cost of the wall," a reference to the $12–66.9 billion border barrier being proposed by President Trump, or compared to $19.4 billion, the 2016 cost of border enforcement in the US. Nazario reports on an integrated set of schemes in Rivera Hernández, the most violent neighborhood in San Pedro Sula, the "murder capital of the world for four years running." Over a two-year period, the programs reduced by 77 percent the risk of criminal offending or alcohol or drug abuse by the targeted youth compared to untargeted peers. The violence prevention program also increased conviction rates for those charged with homicide in the neighborhood, from a low of 4 percent (because of the fear of murderous retaliation) to a new record of over 50 percent. During the same period, killings had decreased by 62 percent. Most significant for my argument, over the same two-year period, the violence prevention program reduced by over half the number of Honduran youth arriving at the US/ Mexico border.[9]

Well-planned social and economic development, coupled with more equitable trade policies, fairer tax regimes, protection of the rule of law, and good and stable governance, ultimately lead to more prosperity, education, and skill development. Expanded social protection schemes, such as those just described, constitute a more just, rational, and cost effective way of reducing the pressures to embark on distress migration than coercive border controls.

In addition to capacious and well-targeted social protection, the expansion of rights-compliant work permit schemes and other means for promoting legal labor migration across regions, including multi-year and multi-entry visas, are part of the answer to the current humanitarian crisis. Unskilled and semi-skilled workers in particular should be included in schemes to reduce inequality and promote access to opportunity. Some very large programs promote limited forms of mobility and income generation, but fail as transformative or redistributive tools, because they severely limit earnings, health, and other benefits, and deny opportunities for workers to bring their families to live with them. This is the case for the unskilled and seasonal visas issued by the US government.

Similarly restrictive terms apply to the more than 1 million work permit or Kafala awardees in the United Arab Emirates already discussed earlier, where a system of virtual apartheid between some of the richest and some of the poorest populations in the world cohabiting in close proximity persists. Given that 90 percent of the country's workforce consists of migrant South Asian workers who are denied the right to unionize or to ever settle or acquire Emirati citizenship, who have very limited access to quality health care and highly restricted upward mobility, these schemes, while affording access to higher wages than would be available back home, perpetuate troubling race, class, and nationality-based segregation, and fuel the unequal global economic system of production and consumption. In part, these schemes are an indictment of the migrant workers' governments that have failed to ensure rights-based employment standards. Some large worker-exporting countries such as the Philippines, and to a lesser extent Indonesia, provide good examples of much more vigorous engagement with the protection of their overseas working citizens, insisting on minimum health care, pay, and working hour and holiday standards, with positive consequences. At a minimum, migrant worker schemes should include these basic worker rights protections.

The success of migrant worker schemes as measures enhancing social justice depends on rigorous enforcement of minimum wage standards, and health and safety regulations in the Global North workplaces that depend on these schemes. Dramatic demographic changes already under way will only increase the relevance of these considerations.

Demography

On current demographic trends, youthful migration will be essential for countries as different as Germany, Canada, and Australia. In 2015, for the first time ever, the global proportion of elderly people aged 65 and over surpassed that of children aged between 0 and 14. By 2025, nearly a quarter of the EU citizenry will be over 65; the increase in the over 85s will be particularly steep. Experts predict that the size of the elderly population in 2060 will be nearly double what it was in 2010 and that the share of people over 80 will rise to 12 percent of the population.[10]

Demographic changes at the opposite end of the

age spectrum are also significant. Many EU member states have sharply declining birth rates, some below the rate of replacement. In 2015, the total fertility rate (TFR, or births per woman) was 1.3 for Spain and 1.4 for Italy. By contrast, other regions of the world, particularly sub-Saharan Africa, exhibit the opposite birth rate trend. The TFR for Sudan during the same period was 4.3, and for Somalia 6.4.

One consequence of this demographic trend is captured by the potential support ratio (PSR), the ratio of the working age population to those aged 65 and over. In 1950, the global PSR was 12:1; today it has declined to 8:1 and by 2050 it is projected to decline to 4:1 – only four workers per elderly non-worker. But this global picture conceals dramatic regional variations. By 2050 in countries like Germany and Italy, PSRs are expected to fall to 5:1; in Uganda and Nigeria, by contrast, they are expected to be 16:6 and 15:1 respectively.

With a zero net increase in migration, the working age population in Europe will drop by 3.5 percent by 2020; over the next 50 years, it will decline by 42 million. Though the promotion of gender equality and retirement age postponement can also contribute to addressing this decline, immigration undoubtedly constitutes another valuable asset for tackling the demographic challenge ahead.

The UN's Approach to Solving the Refugee and Migration Crisis

As we saw at the beginning of this chapter, the UN has recently embarked on a program of action to address current migration challenges. Its central proposal, announced in September 2016, is the creation of two new "Global Compacts," to be developed by 2018, one centered on refugee policy, the other focused on the development of a new framework for managing global migration.[11]

A central target is to "Facilitate orderly, safe, regular and responsible migration and mobility of people." Success in realizing this target will depend on extensive political support and vigorous engagement with many aspects of the drivers of migration discussed above. The Declaration launching the Global Compacts (referred to as the New York Declaration) has called for "a strengthened humanitarian-development nexus, and improve[d] coordination with peace building efforts."[12] It also calls for the implementation of robust nondiscrimination norms that are "people centered, sensitive, humane, dignified, gender responsive," and for enhanced data collection on migration flows, both laudable and important goals that have so far remained elusive. More energetic international collaboration on border control to tackle transnational organized crime, terrorism, and other security threats is also likely.

The New York Declaration also calls for increased sharing of the responsibility for receiving and hosting refugees by states; the expansion of rescue missions at sea and humanitarian temporary evacuation programs where needed; increased funding of humanitarian support in "first host countries," those neighboring the exodus countries, and efforts to stimulate refugee self-sufficiency with meaningful educational and employment opportunities through both public and private investment.[13]

The Declaration reiterates the now widely accepted and welcome commitment to move away from camps as the default strategy for delivering assistance to refugees, in favor of a less segregated approach. This policy recognizes the devastating consequences of protracted encampment for refugees and the de facto choice by more than 60 percent of the global refugee population to live outside camps, increasingly in urban settings. We cannot solve the refugee crisis by fencing people off in desolate camps for decades, the clearest evidence of what Derek Gregory has called our "colonial present"[14] or by denying a means of self-sufficient livelihood to populations eager to rebuild their lives.[15]

As regards non-refugee migration, the New York Declaration calls for an expansion of visas for workers, for skill training, and for family reunification. Positive reference is also made to recent initiatives to protect and give voice to migrants in countries experiencing conflict or natural disaster (the so-called "Migrants in Countries in Conflict," or MICIC initiative) and to enhance disaster risk preparedness, displacement assistance, and more long-term solutions for those displaced by climate change (the so-called Nansen Initiative and its successor, the 2016 Platform on Disaster Displacement).[16]

These laudable goals for the reform process at high level touch on several of the substantive challenges posed by the refugee and migration crisis, and go well beyond the immediate symptoms of refugee and migration distress.

Toward a Rights-Based Refugee and Migration Management System

If, as I argue, the primary drivers of distress migration are conflict, natural disasters and climate change, global inequality and demographic changes, then no solution to the current refugee and migration crisis can be found solely by addressing its most evident symptoms, critical though they are.

I have suggested that the many initiatives to build new refugee and migration management systems, including through the UN Global Compact process, are essential. From the perspective of our humanitarian obligations to others in need, a bedrock of religious and ethical norms across societies and cultures, as Chapter 2 noted, we urgently need to improve our safety net to protect those fleeing violence and other serious threats to life and freedom. This entails more vigorous, generous, and consistent engagement with distress migration, not only through a revivified Refugee Convention but more broadly, as discussed above.

We also need dramatically improved mechanisms for ensuring rescue at sea, for allocating exit visas and generating humanitarian escape corridors. As recent European developments have shown, these measures will only be sustainable if they are accompanied by domestic preparedness that defuses native resentment and fear, with substantial investment in internal provision to accommodate new arrivals and accompany them during the inevitable 5–10-year transitional period until they become self-sufficient. Given the relative youth, vigor, and ambition of the distress migrant population, this is not an open-ended commitment but a wise invest-ment in supporting a population likely to contribute much more than it costs within a decade of arrival.

Closely linked to these border management and post entry mechanisms are urgent reforms to increase collective responsibility sharing across the Global North, whether according to the metric developed by the European Commission based on a territory/population density/GDP ratio or some other agreed formula. The example of Canada, where refugee sponsorship by citizens has generated thousands of openings for refugee resettlement, is a powerful one that could be emulated much more broadly. Sanctuary cities across the US and Sweden also attempt to develop public–private partnerships that generate support and hospitality to supplement government schemes. Within the EU, much more vigorous relocation from the over-taxed countries of the southern Mediterranean, especially Greece and Italy, is urgently needed. In May 2015, the European Council proposed measures to relocate 40,000 migrants in July and, in September, another 120,000. But by February 2016, member states had only allocated 4,522 relocation places. This reloca-tion failure has resulted in the de facto entrapment of hundreds of thousands of migrants and refugees in those ill-equipped border countries.

Impressive outpourings of popular support for distress migrants in need of neighborly assistance need to be marshaled by determined and skillful political leadership to outmaneuver the xenophobic hatred in evidence today. Outside the Global North, humanitarianism – but also security and collective economic self-interest – require an enhanced investment in the safety and economic and social well-being of displaced populations. The disastrous neglect of recent years, and the effects it has provoked, including in terms of sizeable population outflows to the Global North, have now, belatedly, given rise to a series of refugee response plans that outline detailed strategies for the provision of much needed services. Creative thought is also being given to mechanisms for enhancing the self-sufficiency of distress migrant populations, through initiatives such as public–private partnerships, land redistribution schemes, and a variety of other creative development initiatives. All these are urgently needed and welcome, provided they do not entail the creation of exploitative "enterprise zones" with poor labor conditions that trap people who want to move on.

Humanitarian interventions alone will not solve the current refugee and migration situation. As I have indicated, much more capacious, flexible, and inclusive legal means for stimulating and supporting human mobility need to be instituted. These include an expansion of work permits, especially for unskilled or semi-skilled labor, with the aim of replacing the large populations of highly exploited irregular migrants who currently perform unskilled work, with workers in safe and rights respecting employment situations. Environmental dislocation and demographic shifts will make these schemes more and more necessary.

Finally, and perhaps most critically of all, serious attention needs to be paid to a collective engagement with the needs of the next generation, growing up in situations where the prospects of a rights-filled and rewarding life are increasingly elusive. Already now, rough estimates suggest that approximately 15 percent of the 232 million contemporary international migrants are under the age of 20. The proportion for refugees is much higher – children constitute over half the world's refugees. Across the world, in rural and economically depressed regions within generally prosperous states, as the Arab Spring brought starkly to notice, a demographic explosion of young people is not matched by commensurate opportunities for higher education, skill training, and, above all, employment.[17] The same is true across many parts of sub-Saharan Africa, Latin America, and Eastern Europe.

In very large numbers, children and young people are trapped in oppressively exploitative situations, as participants in child labor, sexual exploitation, armed conflict, and a range of forms of trafficking. Though by no means all these children move far from their homes, many do, and significant numbers experience traumatic forms of migration, either duped by traffickers or otherwise subjected to intolerable forms of child abuse and persecution. The absence of strong domestic child protection mechanisms and educational and employment opportunities at home is compounded by the dramatic dearth of protective measures for children in the migration and refugee contexts.

So, serious attention needs to be paid to the needs and rights of the next generation. What should this attention consist of? Most central is the redistribution of educational and employment opportunity, to match the aspirations for self-advancement of all young people and give a fair chance to those currently forced out of school or never given adequate access to quality schooling (leading to employment) in the first place. A plethora of possibilities exist. Demographic shifts are freeing up educational spaces in the Global North, which could and should be put to the service of underserved constituencies.

There are two ways of doing this. One is by instituting much more capacious educational mobility, not just for wealthy populations as currently exists for elites attending boarding schools and high-quality tertiary educational establishments far from home, but for a much broader range of students. Student visas accompanied by scholarships or loan schemes could ensure that very large numbers of young people benefit from educational opportunity, enhancing their prospects of employment. A significant expansion of flexible student visas accompanied by scholarships and development-funded schemes is called for. Development budgets could include earmarked line items for these programs, including an injection of scholarship funds for educational institutions in the Global North.

An excellent precedent exists – the EU Erasmus Program. Established in 1987 and replaced by Erasmus+ in 2014, this has been a tremendously popular and successful student mobility scheme. Not only has it greatly contributed to the creation of a cosmopolitan and open-minded European identity, one not hamstrung by nationalist prejudices or cultural insularity, but it has acted as a powerful redistributive mechanism, affording students from poorer countries previously unimaginable opportunities to study in some of the best centers for higher education in Europe. In the 30 years that Erasmus has existed, there have been 9 million participants. Between 2007 and 2013, outward student mobility doubled in Hungary, Turkey, and Cyprus due to Erasmus, with countries such as Slovakia and Montenegro seeing growth in mobility in excess of 75 percent. Poland, Turkey, and Romania have benefited most from teacher training in Western Europe.[18] The Erasmus+ program has a budget of more than €18 billion (for the period 2014–20), allocated from member state contributions.[19] There is no reason why this magnificent precedent should not be the model for a global Erasmus scheme.

Just as historic enmities, cultural and linguistic difference between Turkey and Greece, Poland and Germany, Romania and Hungary have been overcome to the great benefit of a new generation of cosmopolitan and educated youth, so the same can and should happen across continents. The racial and cultural differences within Europe loomed as large, even insurmountable, less than a century ago as global differences are today. The span of Erasmus, with millions of Black and Asian Londoners, Turkish Berliners and Moroccan Parisians, covers an area no more culturally, racially, or religiously homogeneous than Europe and the Middle East or Africa combined, or America and Latin America, or Australia and Asia.

A second set of strategies exists for realizing the goal of more equal and just access to educational and employment opportunity for the next generation. Mobile information technology has so far been radically underutilized for the equal distribution of quality education at all levels, particularly at tertiary level. Whereas considerable strides have been made with Tele-Medicine, allowing severely under-resourced areas, such as the West Bank and Gaza (and even war-torn Syria) to benefit, little has been done to make the huge educational resources of quality universities, technical and vocational colleges, and other centers of higher learning more easily accessible to populations in the Global South. With many tertiary educational institutions now developing on-line MOOCs (Massive Open Online Courses) and other curricular innovations, it seems feasible for relatively low investment in programmatic and institutional resources to generate very substantial educational benefit and redistribution returns.

A promising example of how this approach might develop is the Borderless Higher Education for Refugees (BHER) educational initiative which links York University in Toronto with Somali refugee students in protracted exile in the Dadaab Refugee camp in Kenya.[20] Other small examples of good practice that should be much more widely emulated and scaled up are the Pan African e-Network, a partnership between the Indian government and the African Union to support tele-education initiatives between Africa and India, a partnership that now links seven Indian universities and five African ones. Middlesex University in the UK has a partnership offering e-learning modules to the Islamic University in Gaza, and doctors from Yale University Medical School are offering mental health education and training to NGOs serving Syrian refugees. These small initiatives merit much more attention, investment, and emulation.

None of the many reforms I suggest will fix the refugee and migration crisis alone. But in combination, and with concerted efforts to reduce the drivers of global conflict, to preempt the risk of humanitarian and natural disasters, to systematically engage with global inequality of income, educational, and employment opportunity, and to take stock of demographic trends in a transparent and constructive way, we can go a very long way to radically reducing the rate of contemporary distress migration and its devastating human consequences.

Further Reading

For readers interested in exploring in more detail the history of global migration that I summarize in Chapter 1, there are several excellent options. A good starting place is the concise, readable, and highly informative book by Christiane Harzig and Dirk Hoerder entitled *What is Migration History?* (Cambridge: Polity, 2009). With impressive economy of language, it manages to cover a vast span of global movement with precision, a cogent radical perspective, and rich contextual explanations useful for readers not fully versed in global history.

Two other books also have a global range. One is Patrick Manning's *Migration in World History* (Abingdon: Routledge, 2013), a meticulous, chronological account of human mobility, which starts with human prehistory and the development of agriculture and of land and water transport, and continues through the Middle Ages and Early Modern Period right up to the contemporary era. Another, quite eye-opening work is the rich inter-disciplinary volume *Migration History in World History: Multidisciplinary Approaches*, edited by Jan Lucassen, Leo Lucassen, and Patrick Manning (Leiden, Boston: Brill, 2010). This book pro-vides the reader with a fascinating compilation of migration-related research findings by eminent linguists, archeologists, biologists, psychologists, and anthropologists. It shows, for example, how careful analysis of human skeletal remains and the plant traces in them can reveal migratory routes, and how careful analysis of linguistic appropriation and transformation provide evidence of antecedent human mobility.

I recommend three other country- or region-specific works, among a plethora of options, for readers interested in delving into the deeper his-tory of particular areas. Each of them is superb in its own way. One is Adam McKeown's article "Global Migration, 1846–1940" (*Journal of World History* 15/2, 2004, pp. 155–189), which makes a compelling case for revising the orthodox account of human migration to take account of Asian flows that, he argues, are every bit as significant in scale and import as the Euro-American migrations that have attracted the lion's share of scholarly comment. McKeown's erudition about Chinese history and his incisive thinking about the determinants of human mobility constitute a critical revision to the established canon. A marvelous history of a particular chapter of human forced migration, which illustrates the tragic and enduring consequences of enforcing ethnic and religious uniformity on state populations, is Bruce Clark's *Twice a Stranger: The Mass Expulsions that Forged Modern Greece and Turkey* (Cambridge, MA: Harvard University Press, 2006). Finally, for readers interested in both the big picture of the largest ever forced migration in human history (affecting about 40 million people) and the complex personal calculations that determine individual human choices about staying or leaving in excruciating circumstances, I recommend Joya Chatterji's masterful account of one aspect of the partition of British India: *The Spoils of Partition: Bengal and India, 1947–1967* (Cambridge: Cambridge University Press, 2007).

There is an extensive literature on the ethical questions relevant to the duties owed to strangers. Much of this work centers on duties owed to impoverished or otherwise disadvantaged populations generally, whether they are in one's own country or abroad. A classic in this field, which addresses the tension between the severity of need of the stranger and the proximity of his or her relationship to the benefactor, is Henry Shue's "Mediating Duties" (*Ethics* 98/4, 1998, pp. 687–704). I make use of some of Shue's powerful metaphors to highlight the dilemma he discusses.

Only a small portion of the writing on the ethics of care to others directly focuses on the obligations toward refugees and migrants that I discuss in Chapter 2. Within that body of work, a landmark contribution is Joseph Carens, *The Ethics of Immigration* (Oxford: Oxford University Press, 2013). Carens presents the most cogent and consistent argument in favor of a generous, open, and inclusive approach to immigration.

A book that combines in-depth knowledge of migration and refugee law with sophisticated political theory is Linda Bosniak's commendably lucid *The Citizen and the Alien: Dilemmas of Contemporary Membership* (Princeton: Princeton University Press, 2006). The book not only includes a careful discussion of relevant ethical arguments advanced by leading political theorists such as John Rawls and Michael Walzer, but it illuminatingly relates their abstract concepts of duties and membership to concrete situations litigated in immigration case law.

Another erudite but highly readable and compelling book about the responsibilities owed to non-citizens is Seyla Benhabib's *The Rights of Others: Aliens, Residents and Citizens* (Cambridge: Cambridge University Press, 2004). In elegant prose, Benhabib engages with the philosopher Immanuel Kant's famous theory of the categorical imperative to reveal its compelling relevance to our contemporary dilemmas. She also advances an interesting and critical discussion of the work of the famous Jewish theorist of the "banality of evil," Hannah Arendt, questioning Arendt's deep skepticism about the power of international structures to protect refugees from their own state's barbarism.

A useful compilation for readers interested in differing perspectives on free movement across borders is Brian Barry and Robert E. Goodwin's edited volume *Free Movement: Ethical Issues in the Transnational Migration of People and Money* (University Park, PA: Penn State University Press, 1992). Finally, Itamar Mann's excellent book *Humanity at Sea: Maritime Migration and the Foundations of International Law* (Cambridge: Cambridge University Press, 2016) probes the ethical challenges that arise when we confront life and death choices – as with distress migrants who are stranded at sea or on the verge of drowning. The book starts with Jews fleeing the Holocaust and ends with Syrians fleeing the country's murderous conflict. In a timely inquiry into the powerful impact of real time images of human suffering, Mann illuminates the complex intersection of international legal norms and emotional pressures as drivers of policy.

On Chapter 3 and the workings of national border control as the basis for migration and refugee systems, a foundational text is John Torpey's classic book *The Invention of the Passport: Surveillance, Citizenship and the State* (Cambridge: Cambridge University Press, 2000). Other useful accounts of the development of policies and practices for managing refugee and migration flows are Matthew J. Gibney, *The Ethics and Politics of Asylum: Liberal Democracy and the Response to Refugees* (Cambridge: Cambridge University Press, 2004), Frances Stonor Saunders, "Where On Earth Are You?" (*London Review of Books* 38/5, March 3, 2016, pp. 7–12), and the European Commission, *A European Agenda on Migration*, May 13, COM(2015) 240, pp. 1–22. My own book, *Child Migration and Human Rights in a Global Age* (Princeton: Princeton University Press, 2014) provides a comprehensive account of the workings and impact of global migration and refugee policy from the perspective of children.

An influential book on the important links between migration and refugee policy on the one hand and development related issues on the other is Alexander Betts, *Survival Migration: Failed Governance and the Crisis of Displacement* (Ithaca, NY: Cornell University Press, 2013). Noted development economist Paul Collier's *Exodus: How Migration is Changing Our World* (Oxford: Oxford University Press, 2013) is an opinionated and provocative account of drivers of migration in a grossly unequal global economic order. Another powerful account of the impact of Western policy failure on refugee populations is the moving book by Jennifer Hyndman and Wenona Giles, *Refugees in Extended Exile: Living on the Edge* (Abingdon, UK: Routledge, 2017). An in-depth but readable case study of the impact of current refugee and migration policies on a particularly vulnerable population, unaccompanied child migrants and refugees, is Vasileia Digidiki and Jacqueline Bhabha's *Emergency Within an Emergency: The Growing Epidemic of Sexual Exploitation and Abuse of Migrant Children in Greece* (Cambridge, MA: Harvard FXB Center for Health and Human Rights, 2017; https://cdn2.sph.harvard.edu/wp-content/uploads/sites/5/2017/04/Emergency-Within-an-Emergency-FXB.pdf).

The question of viable and humane next steps for

solving the refugee and migration crisis discussed in Chapter 4 has generated a considerable literature. Much of the best work on the development of migration and refugee policies, generally highly readable and not jargon-filled, is being conducted under the auspices of specialist think tanks or the mandates of UN experts. In this connection, reports produced by the Migration Policy Institute (www.migration policy.org) are of uniformly high quality and worth consulting for topics of special interest (such as the development of educational policy for migrants, or good models for refugee sponsorship systems or the future development of work permit schemes). The reports produced by the UN Special Rapporteur on the Human Rights of Migrants, François Crépeau, contain forward-looking, progressive and insightful observations and recommendations (www. ohchr.org/EN/Issues/Migration/SRMigrants). Also highly relevant to the broader issues at stake in finding a solution to the migration and refugee crisis is *Reconstructing Atrocity Prevention*, edited by Sheri P. Rosenberg, Tibi Galis, and Alex Zucker (Cambridge: Cambridge University Press, 2016). This excellent volume brings together a rich collection of articles that tackle the daunting challenge of addressing some of the main precipitators of distress migration. For readers interested in exploring the future of refugee and migration management, two papers provide fascinating and accessible material. One is the *New York Declaration for Refugees and Migrants*, agreed by the member states of the United Nations at the General Assembly in September 2016, a powerful international document that sets the stage for the creation of two new Global Compacts by 2018, one on refugees and one on migrants (http://www.un.org/ga/search/view_doc.asp?symbol=A/71/L.1). The other, focused on Europe but with wide-ranging and progressive ideas applicable more broadly, is by François Crépeau and Anna Purkey, "Facilitating Mobility and Fostering Diversity: Getting European Migration Governance to Respect the Human Rights of Migrants" (*CEPS Paper in Liberty and Security in Europe* 92, May 2016).

As I note in this book, the refugee and migration crisis has spawned a huge cultural response, spanning literature, film, music, and art. Among a host of powerful general books on the topic, a few are particularly noteworthy. One, written over a decade ago but that still provides one of the most compelling accounts of distress migration, is Caroline Moorehead's *Human Cargo* (London: Chatto and Windus, 2005). More recent additions are the vivid account by the first ever migration journalist,

Further Reading

Patrick Kingsley, in his *The New Odyssey: The Story of Europe's Refugee Crisis* (Guardian Books, London: Faber and Faber, 2016), noted author of *The Reluctant Fundamentalist* Mohsin Hamid's *Exit West* (London: Penguin, 2017) and Viet Thanh Nguyen's collection, *The Refugees* (New York: Grove Atlantic, 2017).

.

Notes

Preface

1 In the following pages, I will use the term "distress migration" to cover the large-scale migration flows, of both refugees and others, that are precipitated by home situations considered intolerable by those leaving and that generate a sense of crisis in host societies. I will define the term in Chapter 3 and contrast its scope with other widely used terms.

Chapter 1 A Crisis Like No Other?

1 Laura Henderson, "What It Means to Say 'Crisis' in Politics and Law"; http://www.e-ir.info/2014/03/05/what-it-means-to-say-crisis-in-politics-and-law/.

2 See, for example, Makau Mutua, *Human Rights: A Political and Cultural Critique* (Philadelphia: Pennsylvania University Press, 2002), pp. 10–70.

3 Adam McKeown, "A World Made Many: Integration

and Segregation in Global Migration, 1840–1940," *Journal of World History* 15/2, 2004, p. 50.

4 Jared Diamond, *Guns Germs and Steel: The Fates of Human Societies* (New York, London: W.W.Norton & Co. 2005[1997]), pp. 344–345.

5 Benedict Anderson, *Imagined Communities* (London: Verso, 1983).

6 Patrick Manning, *Migration in World History*, 2nd edn. (Abingdon, UK: Routledge, 2013), p. 19. Much of the following discussion is heavily indebted to Manning's influential work on this topic.

7 Shomarka Keita, "Migration in Biological Anthropology," in Jan Lucassen, Leo Lucassen and Patrick Manning (eds.), *Migration History in World History: Multidisciplinary Approaches* (Leiden, Boston: Brill, 2010), pp. 62–68.

8 McKeown, "A World Made Many," p. 42.

9 *The Telegraph* (November 6, 2007): http://www.telegraph.co.uk/comment/3643823/Enoch-Powells-Rivers-of-Blood-speech.html.

10 Manning, *Migration in World History*, p. 154.

11 McKeown, "A World Made Many," p. 44–45.

12 Christiane Harzig and Dirk Hoerder, *What Is Migration History?* (Cambridge: Polity, 2009), p. 43.

13 Joya Chatterji, *The Spoils of War* (Cambridge: Cambridge University Press, 2006), p. 118.

14 I owe this insight to Tara Zahra, who graciously shared an unpublished draft paper exploring a related idea with me.

Chapter 2   A Duty of Care

1 The child was first referred to as Aylan Kurdi, but it later emerged that Alan was his name.

2 Noted in Itamar Mann, *Humanity at Sea* (Cambridge: Cambridge University Press, 2016), p. 1.

3 Coincidentally there is a Canadian connection to this incident too – Phan Kim Phúc is now a Canadian citizen. Unlike Alan, she survived her ordeal and lives in Canada.

4 *New York Times* (September 3, 2015): https://www. nytimes.com/2015/09/04/world/europe/hungarian-le ader-rebuked-for-saying-muslim-migrants-must-be-bl ocked-to-keep-europe-christian.html (italics added).

5 *Washington Post* (September 3, 2015): https://www. washingtonpost.com/news/worldviews/wp/2015/09/ 03/image-of-drowned-syrian-toddler-aylan-kurdi-jolts-world-leaders/?utm_term=.0ed0ec18e2b0.

6 EC Press Release: http://europa.eu/rapid/press-release_SPEECH-15-5614_en.htm

7 *New York Times* (September 5, 2015): https://www. nytimes.com/2015/09/06/world/gulf-monarchies-bristle-at-criticism-over-response-to-syrian-refugee-crisis.html

8 http://foreignpolicy.com/2016/02/26/china-host-syri an-islam-refugee-crisis-migrant/.

9 Henry Shue, "Mediating Duties," *Ethics* 98/4, 1988, pp. 687–704.

10 Michael Walzer, *Spheres of Justice: A Defense of Pluralism and Equality* (1983), cited in Linda Bosniak, *The Citizen and the Alien: Dilemmas of*

Contemporary Membership (Princeton: Princeton University Press, 2006), p. 40.

11 Immanuel Kant, *Perpetual Peace* (1795), cited in Seyla Benhabib, *The Rights of Others: Aliens, Residents and Citizens* (Cambridge: Cambridge University Press, 2004), p. 26.

12 Joseph H. Carens, *The Ethics of Immigration* (Oxford: Oxford University Press, 2013), p. 239.

13 Thomas Lacqueur, "Bodies, Details and the Humanitarian Narrative," in Lynn Hunt (ed.), *The New Cultural History* (Berkeley, University of California Press, 1989), p. 178. I am grateful to Seth Koven for pointing me to this article.

14 Itamar Mann, *Humanity at Sea: Maritime Migration and the Foundations of International Law* (Cambridge, Cambridge University Press, 2016), p. 12.

Chapter 3   The System at Breaking Point

1 The White House (November 20, 2014): https://obamawhitehouse.archives.gov/the-press-office/2014/11/20/remarks-president-address-nation-immigration.

2 *The Daily Express* (February 9, 2017): http://www.express.co.uk/news/world/765172/Geert-Wilders-European-Union-referendum-Nexit-Dutch-election.

3 John Maynard Keynes, "National Self-Sufficiency," in *Collected Writings*, ed. Donald Moggridge (London: Macmillan, 1982), cited in Brian Barry and Robert E. Goodwin (eds.), *Free Movement: Ethical*

Issues in the Transnational Migration of People and Money (University Park, PA: Penn State University Press, 1992), p. 10.

4 Refugee flight is the forced movement of persons defined as refugees by Art. 1(a) of the 1951 *UN Convention on the Status of Refugees*. The definition and its scope are discussed later in this chapter.

5 Alexander Betts, *Survival Migration: Failed Governance and the Crisis of Displacement* (Ithaca, NY: Cornell University Press, 2013), pp. 4–5.

6 Quoted in Robert E. Goodwin, "If People were Money," in Barry and Goodwin, *Free Movement*, p. 13.

7 Cited in Matthew Gibney, *The Ethics and Politics of Asylum: Liberal Democracy and the Response to Refugees* (Cambridge: Cambridge University Press, 2004), pp. 169–170.

8 Giorgio Agamben, *Homo Sacer: Sovereign Power and Bare Life* (Stanford: Stanford University Press, 1998), p. 17.

9 Gibney, *The Ethics and Politics of Asylum*, p. 129.

10 1951 *UN Convention on the Status of Refugees*, Art. 1(a).

Chapter 4 Finding Workable and Humane Solutions

1 I am grateful to Kathryn Sikkink for insisting on this point in a discussion.

2 Center for Systemic Peace (2016), *Major Episodes of Political Violence, 1946–2016*: http://www.sys temicpeace.org/warlist/warlist.htm; Peace Research

Institute Oslo (2016), *Trends in Armed Conflict, 1946–2015*: http://files.prio.org/Publication_files/prio/Dupuy%20et%20al%20-%20Trends%20in%20Armed%20Conflict%201946-2015,%20Conflict%20Trends%208-2016.pdf.

3 UNHCR and Global Monitoring Report (2016), cited in Sarah Dryden Peterson, "Refugee Education: The Crossroads of Globalization," *Educational Research* 43/9, 2016, p. 474.

4 Paul Collier, *Exodus: How Migration is Changing Our World* (Oxford: Oxford University Press, 2013), p. 271.

5 Kathleen Newland, "Migration as a factor in Development and Poverty Reduction," June 1, 2003, Migration Policy Institute; http://www.migrationpolicy.org/article/migration-factor-development-and-poverty-reduction

6 John Gibson, David McKenzie, Halahingano Rohorua, and Steven Stillman, "The Long-Term Impacts of International Migration: Evidence from a Lottery," World Bank Policy Research Working Paper No. 7495, 2015; https://ideas.repec.org/p/wbk/wbrwps/7495.html.

7 UNDP, *International Migration Report*, 2015, p. 2.

8 Guy Stecklov, Paul Winters, Marco Stampini, and Benjamin Davis, "Do Conditional Cash Transfers Influence Migration? A Study Using Experimental Data from the Mexican PROGRESA Program," *Demography* 42/4, 2005, pp. 769–790.

9 Sonia Navarro, "How to Secure the Border: Spoiler Alert: A Wall Won't Do It." OpEd, *LA Times*, April

23, 2017; http://www.latimes.com/opinion/op-ed/
la-oe-nazario-what-works-to-end-illegal-immigrati
on-20170423-story.html. For a useful discussion
of the utility of adopting a cost of inaction framework, see Sudhir Anand et al., *The Cost of Inaction*
(Cambridge, MA: Harvard University Press, 2012).

10 European Commission, cited in François Crépeau and
Anna Purkey, "Facilitating Mobility and Fostering
Diversity: Getting European Migration Governance
to Respect the Human Rights of Migrants," *CEPS
Paper in Liberty and Security in Europe* 92, May
2016, p. 30.

11 UN General Assembly, *New York Declaration for
Refugees and Migrants*, A/71/150 (September 15,
2016).

12 UN General Assembly, *New York Declaration for
Refugees and Migrants*, A/71/150 (September 15,
2016), para 37.

13 For examples of what is likely to be developed and
strengthened, see UNHCR, *Regional Refugee and
Migrant Response Plan for Europe*, January to
December 2017: http://knowledge.unccd.int/publi
cations/regional-refugee-and-migrant-response-plan-
europe-january-december-2017.

14 Derek Gregory, *The Colonial Present: Afghanistan,
Palestine and Iraq* (Oxford: Blackwell Publishing,
2004), cited in Jennifer Hyndman and Wenona Giles,
Refugees in Extended Exile: Living on the Edge
(Abingdon and Oxford: Routledge. 2017), p. xv.

15 For excellent proposals on promoting refugee self-
sufficiency, see Karen Jacobsen and Susan Fratzke,

"Building Livelihood Opportunities for Refugee Populations: Lessons from Past Practice" (2017); http://www.migrationpolicy.org/research/building-li velihood-opportunities-refugee-populations-lessons -past-practice.

16 See the 2014 Guidelines to Protect Migrants in Countries Experiencing Conflict or Natural Disaster: https://micicinitiative.iom.int/about-micic. See also the October 2012 Nansen Initiative launched by the governments of Switzerland and Norway to build consensus among states about how best to address cross-border displacement in the context of sudden- and slow-onset disasters: Development and Cooperation (2017), *The Nansen Initiative's Protection Agenda*: https://www.dandc.eu/en/arti cle/nansen-initiatives-protection-agenda-what-do-ab out-disaster-displacement. See also Development and Cooperation (2017), *The Needs of Displaced Persons*: https://www.dandc.eu/en/article/forced-dis placement-related-disasters-one-great-humanitarian-challenges-21st-century.

17 UNDP, *Arab Human Development Report 2016: Youth and the Prospects for Human Development in a Changing Reality*; www.undp.org/rbas.

18 European Commission (2017), The 30th Anniversary; https://ec.europa.eu/programmes/erasmus-plus/anni versary/30th-anniversary-and-you_en

19 European Commission (2016), Erasmus+ Annual Report 2015; https://ec.europa.eu/programmes/ erasmus-plus/sites/erasmusplus/files/erasmus-plus-annual-report-2015.pdf.

20 Wenona Giles and Aida Orgocka, "Imagining a Future through Education: Adolescents in Extended Exile in Dadaab," in Jacqueline Bhabha, Daniel Senovilla Hernández, and Jyothi Kanics (eds.), *Research Handbook on Child Migration* (Wakefield, UK: Edward Elgar Press, forthcoming 2018).